Matthew

Books in the Bible Study Commentary Series

BIBLE STUDY COMMENTARY

Matthew

HOWARD F. VOS

Lamplighter Books Grand Rapids, Michigan
Zondervan Publishing House

Matthew: A Bible Study Commentary
© 1979 by Howard F. Vos

Lamplighter Books are published by Zondervan
Publishing House, 1415 Lake Drive, S.E.,
Grand Rapids, Michigan 49506

Library of Congress Cataloging in Publication Data

Vos, Howard Frederic, 1925–
    Matthew, a study guide commentary.
    Bibliography: p.
      1. Bible. N.T. Matthew—Study.   I. Title
BS2576.V67   226'.2'07   78-31099
ISBN 0-310-33883-2

Printed in the United States of America

86 87 88 89 90 91 92 / 10 9 8 7 6 5 4

Contents

Matthew

Background

The peoples of the world stretch out their hands to make contact with God. In their sense of inadequacy they seek a higher being to strengthen, comfort, and give wisdom. In the insecurity of an ever-changing world with quivering foundations, they search for one who is stable and sure, and who can provide the security all psychologically healthy individuals require.

To the seeking masses of the world, God has sent good news, or the "gospel," which in the New Testament always appears in the singular and applies to *the* preeminent item of good news: God has provided salvation for sinners. This good news is centered in the person and work of Jesus Christ, who came to make salvation possible through His sacrificial death and faith in Him. But the gospel does not stop with the forgiveness of sin, and it is not concerned only with making it possible for sinners to spend eternity with God. Faith in Christ has implications for believers in the present and affects every aspect of their lives. As the Book of Romans clearly teaches, with salvation from sin God has also freely given all other things (Rom. 8:32). This comprehensive divine provision includes everything human beings are looking for: strength, comfort, wisdom, security, purpose, and much more.

The good news about Jesus Christ generally was oral in the earliest days. But in time, written accounts, known as Gospels, recorded the words and deeds of Jesus Christ. The four New Testament Gospels were simply versions of the one gospel, and the names of the writers were attached to the title to distinguish the four books; hence we read "the Gospel According to Matthew" or Mark or Luke or John.

Authorship

The early church fathers unanimously attributed the first Gospel to the apostle Matthew. Since he was an insignificant member of the apostolic band, such an ascription seems unlikely if it were not true. Moreover, all the early manuscripts of the Gospel bear the title "According to Matthew." Though some technical questions about Matthew's authorship have been raised, none are unanswerable.

The Gospel itself makes no claim regarding authorship, but some have found internal indications of Matthew's composition. For instance, Matthew's list of the apostles speaks of "Matthew the tax collector" (10:3), while lists in Mark, Luke, and Acts simply call him Matthew. It has been suggested that the addition of "tax collector" (publican) indicates the author's feeling of his unworthiness to be a member of the Twelve or to write the Gospel. Furthermore, though Matthew, Mark, and Luke all report the feast in Matthew's house after his call to discipleship, Mark and Luke speak of it as taking place in Matthew's house, while Matthew says simply that it took place in "the house."

Several of the early church fathers referred to Matthew's Gospel as having been written in Hebrew (Aramaic). Yet all of them seem to have accepted the Greek Matthew as Matthew's production. Early in the fifth century Jerome put forth the view that the Greek Matthew was a translation of the Aramaic original, but an increasing number of scholars have pointed out that the Gospel as we have it does not bear the marks of a translation. The tendency in many circles today is to conclude that Matthew originally composed his Gospel in Aramaic and that with the passage of time he produced essentially the same message in Greek for a larger audience. This he could easily have done because as a tax collector he would have been bilingual.

If the view is accepted that Matthew originally wrote his Gospel in Aramaic, then undoubtedly he composed it in Palestine, probably between 50 and 55. If he also wrote a Greek Gospel, he must have written it outside Palestine for non-Aramaic-speaking Jews. Where it was written is an open question, but Antioch of Syria is frequently suggested as the place. The date of composition also is uncertain. If the normal prophetic stance of Matthew 24 and 25 is accepted, along with a variety of other hints, the book was written before the Roman destruction of Jerusalem in A.D. 70 and probably before the Jewish revolt broke out in

A.D. 66. Thus the Greek Matthew may have been written between about 55 and 65.

Having said all this about the authorship of the first Gospel, we have not yet dealt with the larger issue of the composition of the Gospels. Authorship of the first four books of the New Testament has baffled scholars because much that is in them is similar and yet much is different. The Gospel of John is so divergent from the others that it usually is treated in a separate category. Such a large percentage of the content of the other three Gospels is alike that they usually are called Synoptics, which means "seeing together," for they see nearly eye to eye concerning many events of the life of Christ.

To illustrate, more than 90 percent of Mark's material appears in both Matthew and Luke, comprising about half of each of those Gospels. Of the remaining 50 percent of the contents of Matthew and Luke, about half is found in both of them; the remainder appears only in one Gospel. On the other hand, less than 10 percent of John is found in all three of the Synoptics.

Among reverent believers down through the ages, it has always been held that God the Holy Spirit desired to emphasize various phases or aspects of the person and work of Christ in the four Gospels, the totality of which would form a reasonably complete picture of what God wanted preserved about the earthly ministry and message of Jesus Christ. In presenting Christ from four points of view or four perspectives, the writers naturally would repeat and diverge in the details of their narratives. The similarity may be explained in at least three ways:

1. There may have been short written accounts of aspects of the work and teachings of Jesus on which all three could have drawn. That there were such written records seems certain (Luke 1:1). But if the writers of the canonical Gospels drew upon them, we should probably expect a more exact verbal correspondence at certain points than we find in the Synoptics.

2. Matthew, Mark, and Luke may have known one another in Jerusalem and/or in Antioch of Syria and may have discussed Christ's earthly ministry on various occasions. This possibility deserves further investigation.

3. Apparently there was an oral tradition about the life and teachings of Christ that circulated in the early church. If Jesus' followers were to present Him properly, they had to tell a consistent story about His

career. And with the constant telling, that story would fall into a rather set pattern. That there was such a common core of accepted truth is indicated in such passages as Luke 1:1-2 ("things . . . believed among us . . . delivered . . . unto us") and 1 Corinthians 15:2-3 ("keep in memory what I preached unto you . . . I delivered unto you . . . that which I also received"). With an oral apostolic tradition there would be some flexibility in order of phrases and words and in emphases, as does in fact occur in the synoptic Gospels. So then, Matthew, Mark, and Luke may have drawn on the body of apostolic oral teaching as it suited their purposes and even may have changed phraseology or emphases as they were led to do under the guidance of the Holy Spirit.

In any case, we must reverently believe that what appears in each of the synoptic Gospels is exactly what the Holy Spirit wanted there. One need not be worried that the disciples were guilty of memory slips in writing about the life of Christ because He promised that the Holy Spirit would "bring all things to your remembrance, whatsoever I have said unto you" (John 14:26) and that He would "teach you all things" (v. 26) and "guide you into all truth" (16:13).

The Message of Matthew

Both the statements of early church writers and the contents of Matthew attest the fact that his special handling of the Good News was designed particularly for Jews. Matthew's Gospel is not a contradiction of Old Testament teachings but a fulfillment of promises made to Abraham and David. It is an apologetic for the messiahship of Christ. This Matthew seeks to demonstrate by reference to Christ's lineage, His deeds, His teachings, and the constant fulfillment of prophecy in His life. Moreover, Matthew stresses the reign of the Messiah; he uses the term *kingdom of heaven* thirty-three times. Reference to the Old Testament is more frequent here than in any of the other Gospels; in all there are about fifty-three quotations from the Old Testament and seventy-six allusions to it. These are drawn from twenty-five Old Testament books.

But Gentiles are also in view in the Book of Matthew. The Magi came from a far country to share in the worship of the newborn Babe of Bethlehem (2:1-12). Two non-Jewish women share in His genealogy (1:5). Matthew is the one Gospel that mentions the church (16:18; 18:17), and it is clear from the Great Commission that more than Jews are to be included in that church (28:19). Moreover, Jesus states specifically that the kingdom will be taken from Israel and given to a people producing the fruits of it (21:43) and that the nations will enter into the inheritance of Israel (8:11-12).

Clearly the Book of Matthew focuses on Christ as the Messiah, the Anointed One who was to come from God to bring deliverance and a new state of divine blessing for His people. In the Old Testament there are many strands of thought concerning the Messiah, but two especially stand out. Preeminently He was to be a king in the Davidic line, but His rule was to be over a kingdom with a utopian character and was to be without termination (2 Sam. 7:4–17). He was to be greater than David— the Son of God Himself (Ps. 2:7). His reign would usher in a new day of peace and righteousness (Isa. 9:2-7). But the Old Testament made it clear that He was also to be a suffering servant of the Lord who would be rejected by His people, would die a substitutionary death for them, and evidently would rise again ("prolong his days," Isa. 53:10). See Isaiah 42:1-9; 49:1-6; 50:4-9; 52:13–53:12.

The people of Jesus' day expected a Messiah. But their thinking was too clouded by Jewish thought of the time, which emphasized Messiah's political power virtually to the exclusion of His spiritual ministry. This is evident even from the comments and attitudes of the disciples, who thought only of His setting up a kingdom and had no conception of a suffering Savior.

In his concentration on Jesus' messiahship, Matthew begins with the lineage and birth of the Messiah-King. Then he proceeds naturally to the ministry of John the Baptist as the herald or forerunner of the King. Next there is the preparation of Jesus Himself through the baptism and temptation. At this point Messiah is ready to begin His ministry and logically does so in His home province of Galilee. Most of chapters 4–13 take place in Galilee, where the Messiah preaches the Sermon on the Mount (chaps. 5–7), attests His messiahship by miraculous works (chaps. 8–12), and delivers the kingdom parables (chap. 13). Then, after a withdrawal from Galilee (chaps. 14–18), He makes His way to Judea, where the rest of the book takes place (chaps. 19–28). After a number of events on the way to Jerusalem, Jesus parries verbal blows with Jewish leaders in the capital and is rejected by them, delivers the great prophetic discourse on the Mount of Olives (chaps. 24–25), suffers the pain of the cross (chaps. 26–27), triumphs in the Resurrection and pronounces the Great Commission (chap. 28). Though the book may be outlined in many ways, a geographical approach is taken here.

Outline

Part One: Messiah's Coming and Preparation (1:1–4:11)
  I. The coming of the Messiah (1:1–2:23)
    A. Birth of the Messiah (1:1-25)
    B. Events of Messiah's infancy (2:1-23)
  II. Preparation for the Messiah's ministry (3:1–4:11)
    A. Ministry of John the Baptist (3:1-12)
    B. Baptism of the Messiah (3:13-17)
    C. Temptation of the Messiah (4:1-11)
Part Two: Messiah's Ministry in Galilee (4:12–18:35)
  I. Beginning of the Messiah's ministry in Galilee (4:12-25)
    A. The unfolding of prophecy (4:12-17)
    B. Call of four disciples (4:18-22)
    C. Jesus' ministry in Galilee (4:23-25)
  II. Principles of the Messiah's kingdom (5:1–7:29)
    A. The Beatitudes (5:1-12)
    B. The influence of the kingdom citizens (5:13-16)
    C. Jesus and the Mosaic law (5:17-48)
    D. False and true piety (6:1-18)
    E. Worldly wealth and cares (6:19-34)
    F. Concluding exhortations to kingdom citizens (7:1-29)
  III. Demonstration of the Messiah's power (8:1–9:34)
    A. First series of miracles (8:1-17)
    B. First response (8:18-22)
    C. Second series of miracles (8:23–9:8)
    D. Second response (9:9-17)
    E. Third series of miracles (9:18-33*a*)
    F. Third response (9:33*b*-34)
  IV. The Messiah and His kingdom preachers (9:35–11:1)
    A. Their call (9:35–10:4)
    B. Their calling (10:5–11:1)
  V. Opposition to the Messiah and His kingdom (11:2–12:50)
    A. Inquiry of John (11:2-19)
    B. Condemnation and commendation (11:20-30)
    C. Confrontation with the Pharisees (12:1-45)
    D. Interference of relatives (12:46-50)
  VI. Parables of the Messiah's kingdom (13:1-52)
    A. Preliminaries to the parables (13:1-2,10-17)

B. Preaching the parables (13:3-9,18-52)
VII. Messiah's withdrawals from Galilee (13:53–18:35)
  A. First withdrawal and the first multiplication of the loaves (13:53–14:36)
  B. Second withdrawal and the second multiplication of the loaves (15:1-39)
  C. Third withdrawal, Peter's confession, and the Transfiguration (16:1–17:23)
  D. Return to Capernaum and instruction of the disciples (17:24–18:35)

Part Three: Messiah's Ministry in Jerusalem (19:1–28:20)
  I. Messiah's journey to Jerusalem (19:1–20:34)
    A. Lessons of life (19:1-26)
    B. Promises and parables (19:27–20:19)
    C. Presumption and persistence (20:20-34)
  II. Messiah's rejection by the Jewish leaders (21:1–23:39)
    A. Reception in Jerusalem (21:1-27)
    B. Pointed parables (21:28–22:14)
    C. Quarrelsome questions (22:15-46)
    D. Warnings and woes (23:1-39)
  III. Messiah's revelation concerning the future (24:1–25:46)
    A. End-time events (24:1-31; 25:31-46)
    B. Applications and Illustrations of the Second Coming (24:32–25:30)
  IV. The Passover of the Messiah (26:1–27:66)
    A. The Last Supper (26:1-35)
    B. Prelude to the crucifixion (26:36–27:26)
    C. The Lord's death and burial (27:27-66)
  V. The triumph of the Messiah (28:1-20)
    A. The Resurrection (28:1-10)
    B. The report of the soldiers (28:11-15)
    C. The Great Commission (28:16-20)

For Further Study

1. Read one or more articles on Matthew the apostle in Bible dictionaries or encyclopedias.

2. If you were to outline Matthew in some way other than the geographical approach, e.g., episodes in the life of Christ, how would you outline it?

3. Make a study of the Old Testament prophecies that Matthew claims were fulfilled in some aspect of the life of Christ.

a. What seems to have been his purpose in making such claims?

b. What specific events or details in the life of Christ are said to have occurred in fulfillment of prophecy?

c. From what Old Testament books do these prophecies come?

PART ONE: *Messiah's Coming and Preparation*

Chapter 1

The Coming of the Messiah
(Matthew 1:1–2:23)

A. Birth of the Messiah (1:1-25)

1. *The family tree of Jesus* (1:1-17). Matthew 1:1 provides a marvelous bridge between the Old Testament and the New. This verse flashes across the memory the great Old Testament figures of Abraham (progenitor of the Hebrews) and David (Israel's great king and empire builder), both recipients of unconditional covenants; and it introduces Jesus Christ, the bringer of the new covenant and the chief personality of the New Testament. The interconnectedness of the two testaments is shown in the fact that Jesus is a descendant of both Abraham and David. Moreover, the verse relates Jesus to the messianic promises (Gen. 12:3; 13:15; 2 Sam. 7:12-13); and the following genealogy demonstrates Jesus' claim to the throne of David—an absolute essential if one were to assert messiahship.

Verse 1 is evidently a title and should properly be regarded as a title of the first seventeen verses. "Book of the generation" might better be translated "family roll" (Lenski), "family tree" (Williams), or "a record of the genealogy" (NIV). Thus it must refer only to verses 1-17, not to the rest of chapter 1 or to the Gospel as a whole, as some assert. The two main ancestors of Jesus—David and Abraham—are listed here. Verses 2-17 provide an elaboration on His ancestry. "Jesus" (*Yahweh is salvation* or *Yahweh saves*) is our Lord's personal name, given at His circumcision (Luke 2:21). It was the name by which He was commonly known while on earth. "Christ" (the equivalent of Hebrew *Messiah,* Anointed One) is the title of His office. The angel used "Christ" as a proper name when announcing Jesus' birth to the shepherds (Luke 2:11), and Jesus used it once or twice (Matt. 23:8,10). The full name "Jesus Christ" came into use only after the Ascension.

Whenever one comes across a genealogy in Scripture, he is tempted to pass quickly over the list of unfamiliar names. But a proper view of the inspiration and authority of the Bible leads to the conclusion that passages such as this are included for a reason. Even a quick reading of this genealogy will reveal some rather surprising things. For instance, though a Jew, Jesus had Gentile blood in His veins—this is significant if He was to be the Savior of the world. Second, the fact that some in the line bore moral blots speaks to us not only of the grace of God in sending a Savior for sinners but also of the degree of humiliation of the Savior in His incarnation (Phil. 2:7-8). Third, it is startling to discover that if this lineage is not modified in some way, Jesus could not be the Messiah because Jechonias (Matt. 1:11) was cursed and was not to have any descendants on the throne. Discussion of this issue appears later.

The genealogy properly begins with Abraham, who was not only the progenitor of the Hebrews but also the recipient of an unconditional covenant. In him all the families of the earth were to be blessed, and to his seed the Land of Promise was to be given forever (Gen. 12:3; 13:15; Gal. 3:16). For two generations the line of promise is single and exclusive, descending through Isaac (Gen. 26:3-4), not Ishmael, and Jacob (Gen. 28:13-14), not Esau. Then the promise broadens to include "Judah and his brothers."[1] Though the reign was to descend through Judah alone, all twelve of the sons of Jacob were heirs of the messianic promise; their descendants would enjoy possession of the Promised Land forever.

In verses 3-6 Matthew takes the unusual step of listing four women, though descent continues through the men. Two of the women were Gentiles (Rahab and Ruth), and three were morally stained (Tamar, see Gen. 38; Rahab the harlot; and the mother of Solomon, Bathsheba). Rahab had been a harlot who was spared during the capture of Jericho and later became a woman of faith (Josh. 2:1; Heb. 11:31). The mention of Bathsheba as "the wife of Uriah" (2 Sam. 11) seems to be a reminder of her sinful relationship with David. As has been suggested, Matthew the publican may have added the touch concerning these sinful women because he was impressed with the grace of God that could reach even

---

[1]Translations of Scripture in this commentary are the author's own unless otherwise specified.

"publicans and harlots" (Matt. 21:31-32). With David the ancestral line reached royalty. And David was rewarded with a covenant which would establish his line and throne forever (2 Sam. 7). Yet this exalted king was fully capable of commiting adultery and murder, implied in the reference to Solomon, "whose mother had been Uriah's wife" (Williams, see 2 Sam. 11-12).

Verses 7-11 contain a list of kings, all of whom appear in 1 Chronicles 3:10-16. But a comparison of the two genealogies shows that for some reason Matthew chose to omit names of four reigning monarchs of Judah: Ahaziah, Joash, Amaziah, and Jehoiakim. Certainly this omission was not a result of ignorance or error on his part because a roster of the kings of Judah was common knowledge and was readily available. Apparently some shortening of the list was necessary for purposes of literary symmetry—to make each grouping come out to fourteen names. This selectivity of names for purposes of symmetry is evident elsewhere in Scripture (see, for instance, Gen. 5 and 11, where there are ten generations from Adam to Noah and ten from Shem to Abraham). Evidently Hebrew genealogical tables are more concerned with demonstrating unbroken descent from father to son than with providing a complete register of pedigree. Such words as *son* and *beget* indicate direct descent but not necessarily immediate descent.

Jechonias (Jeconiah, Coniah, Jehoiachin) and his line were cursed; he was not to have a descendant on the throne (Jer. 22:30; 36:30). But the judgment against Jechonias does not mean that God abrogated the unconditional covenant with David (2 Sam. 7); David could have a descendant on the throne through another branch of the line. Condemnation of Jechonias means that if Jesus were the natural son of Joseph and therefore a descendant of Jechonias, He could not be the Messiah. Therefore the proper conclusion seems to be that Matthew has recorded the genealogy of Joseph, Jesus' legal father, because he was Mary's husband. The genealogy which Luke provides (3:23-38) must then be Mary's genealogy. It traces the line back to David through another son, Nathan, upon whom rested no curse (v. 31); the reference to Joseph as son of Heli (v. 23) would then be understood to mean son-in-law. It is significant to note that the "of whom" in Matthew 1:16 is not plural or masculine singular but feminine singular in the Greek text, pointing up the fact that Jesus was born of Mary. Moreover, the literary structure of the genealogy is broken at verse 16; there is no statement that Joseph "begat" Jesus.

The genealogical list of verses 12-16 does not appear in the Old Testament, and indeed it could not because Scripture is silent for more than four hundred years between Malachi and Matthew. We have no way of knowing whether there are gaps in this part of the line as there were in verses 7-11; very possibly there are. In addition to the confirmed gaps, there are implied gaps because of the unequal time spans involved: from Abraham to David is about a thousand years; from David to the Captivity in Babylon, about four hundred years; and from the Captivity to the birth of Christ, about six hundred years. "Fourteen generations" are thought by many to have been selected for easier memorization. Atkinson observes that the particle *oun*, translated "so" at the beginning of verse 17, implies the artificial arrangement and says, "The sentence means, 'This makes all the generations . . . to be fourteen generations'" (*New Bible Commentary*, p. 774). If one adds up all the names of this genealogy, he gets only forty-one instead of the forty-two required (14 x 3). The problem is most easily solved by counting David twice—at the end of the first list and at the beginning of the second.

2. *The birth of Jesus* (1:18-25). Just as the family tree described here must be Joseph's, so the account of Jesus' birth is presented from Joseph's standpoint. "Now the birth of Jesus Christ was as follows" (NASB) is a theologically valuable statement underscoring the birth of the Messiah as opposed to the false teaching, developed later, that the Messiah entered into Him at baptism.

"Betrothed" is not to be understood in the same sense as the contemporary idea of engagement. Betrothal was the equivalent of actual marriage; it involved the taking of vows before witnesses and required no further ceremony for completion of marriage. Betrothal was followed by a period of some months before the groom brought the bride to his home and celebrated the event with a wedding feast (Matt. 25:1). That betrothal was tantamount to marriage is clear from the fact that verse 19 refers to Joseph as Mary's husband and verse 20 calls Mary Joseph's wife, and that dissolution of the relationship required a formal divorce ("divorce her privately," v. 19).

Before the marriage of Mary and Joseph was consummated by sexual relations, Mary "was found to be with child." How the discovery was made and who told Joseph is not known. Luke 1 intimates that almost immediately after the announcement to Mary that she was to be the mother of the Messiah, she hurried to her cousin Elisabeth for whatever support or consolation she could gain at this very difficult time of her life. Possibly Mary told Joseph something of the details herself on returning to Nazareth. But there is no hint that she tried to explain anything to Joseph; most take the words "by the Holy Spirit" to be Matthew's addition rather than part of Mary's account to Joseph. This phrase asserts the personality and creative power of the Holy Spirit, the innocence of Mary, and the legitimacy of Jesus' birth. Immediately it forestalls any unworthy thoughts about the birth of the Savior.

A betrothed woman who was found unfaithful could be punished by death (Deut. 22:23), but we have no way of knowing how stringently the law was enforced at this point in history. At the minimum, "because Joseph . . . was a righteous man," a truly religious Jew who observed the law, he could not consider finalizing his marriage with a woman guilty of fornication. Two courses were open to him; he could bring Mary before the court to be publicly charged and condemned, or he could put her away privately by drawing up a bill of divorce before two or three witnesses—without even spelling out the charges. His love for Mary led him to take the milder course of action.

After Joseph had brooded over his shattered life for a long while, he fell asleep. In his disturbed condition an angel, perhaps Gabriel himself, appeared to him in a dream. The content of the dream cannot easily be explained away as merely the product of a subconscious desire that now surfaced. This is true because the angel's message conflicted with Joseph's sense of obligation to the law, reversed his decision already made, and set him on a difficult course of action that he would not otherwise have contemplated. Moreover, as Joseph acted by faith on the message of the angel, the sequence of events which unfolded tended to confirm the authenticity of the revelation as a message from God.

"Joseph, son of David" is a princely title and is perhaps a hint that he would have something to do with the birth of Messiah, who should come from the line of David. Joseph was urged to have no fear of taking Mary into his home and giving her his full honor and protection because her child was conceived by the Holy Spirit. That such a statement should have been viewed as sufficient explanation for a simple carpenter of Nazareth is significant, for it implies some knowledge of the divine person of the Spirit on the part of even an ordinary strictly monotheistic Jew.

"You shall call His name Jesus"; God intervenes to dictate the name of Joseph's legal Son. He is not to be named after His legal father or another relative, as would have been customary, but is to be called Jesus, meaning *Yahweh Saves,* because "he will save his people [in the first instance, Jews, but later Gentiles] from their sins," from their penalty as well as their grip on the individual. Thus the angel makes it clear that Jesus as Messiah was to rescue His people from spiritual oppression rather than the political oppression of Rome or the Herods, as popular thinking had come to expect.

It seems natural to conclude that in verses 22 and 23 the angel is still speaking to Joseph. There is no break in the narrative as would be expected if Matthew were stopping to present an observation of his own—under the guidance of the Holy Spirit of course. Moreover, Lenski observes that up to the end of verse 21, "the angel gave no support to Joseph's faith save only his word; but if v. 22, 23 are words of the angel, he would give Joseph the strongest kind of support by citing to him the very promise now being fulfilled" (p. 52).

At any rate, the prophecy being fulfilled is quoted from Isaiah 7:14. Critics often argue that the Hebrew word *'almah,* rendered "virgin" in the Matthew passage, could mean a young woman of marriageable age and need not be viewed as a prophecy of the virgin birth. While it is true that *'almah* may be so translated, in other passages where this word is used in the Old Testament it means virgin. And clearly in this passage the virgin birth is intended. Jesus was born of Mary (v. 16), conceived by the Holy Spirit (v. 20), born of "the virgin" (v. 23); and Joseph had no sexual relations with her until she had given birth to her son (v. 25). Moreover, this son of Mary would be called " 'Immanuel'—which means 'God with us.' " The same angel told Mary that her Son would be called "the Son of God" (Luke 1:35). In other words, this passage (vv. 21-23) teaches the two cardinal doctrines of Christianity: Jesus is the virgin-born Son of God and through Him comes salvation from sin.

When Joseph awoke, he obeyed the command of God. Taking Mary as his wife, he "kept her a virgin until she gave birth to a Son" (NASB), and he called the Son Jesus. "Firstborn" does not appear in the best manuscripts of verse 25. The implication remains, however, that after the birth of Jesus, Joseph and Mary had a normal married life.

These verses provide a bold apologetic to meet the charge that Jesus was the illegitimate offspring of Mary. The fact that Jesus was a Son of Mary, not Joseph, is freely admitted. Then Joseph is brought forward as a witness for Mary. What he did took great courage, but apparently he was fearless in the confidence of the truth of her virginity. His conduct would have been impossible if he had had an insecure hold on the facts. Joseph figures little in the Gospel narrative and often is neglected. But it takes little to imagine what it cost him to give the protection of his spotless reputation and his lineage to Mary and her infant Son. One gets a new appreciation of Joseph as a stalwart of the faith—as a devoted servant of God.

B. Events of Messiah's Infancy (2:1-23)

1. *Visit of the Magi* (2:1-12). Clearly the gospel writers selected material to promote their special view of Jesus. In presenting Him as Messiah-King, Matthew reported His royal lineage. Next he described the visit of Magi from the East to pay homage to the newborn King of the Jews and the worry of Herod the Great over an apparent threat to his rule. The details of Jesus' birth evidently are fairly well known to his readers and do not require retelling here; they figure more largely in the Gospel of Luke, which emphasizes the humanity of Jesus.

The place of Jesus' birth was Bethlehem, about six miles south of Jerusalem. The time was during the reign of Herod the Great (40-4 B.C.), evidently during his last years. It is known that our calendar is in error, but by how much is not clear. Near the end of Herod's reign the Magi came looking for Jesus. The Magi were not kings, as Christian lore has subsequently come to view them, but a class of learned men of Persia or Babylonia. They were experts in the science of their day and dabbled in the occult and especially in astronomy and astrology. Probably these particular Magi came from Babylonia where they had become familiar with the messianic hope through contact with the numerous Jews living there. As Gentiles they hoped to benefit from the reign of the Messiah, especially from the fact that He would bring justice and peace to bless all peoples.

There is plenty of speculation about the star, and treatises have been written on the nature of it. The truth is that no one knows whether it consisted of an unusual conjunction of planets or whether it was some specially prepared stellar phenomenon, possibly even accompanied by a divine revelation. Even if the Magi derived their initial conclusions about the birth of the King of the Jews from astronomical or astrological considerations, it must be admitted that no natural star, millions of miles from earth, can point to a specific structure on earth, as is indicated in verse 9. A special low-hanging astral phenomenon would have been required for that. Moreover, the fact that God directly communicated with the Magi in verse 12 raises the possibility that He had done so earlier.

Their limited knowledge of things naturally led the Magi to go to the Jewish capital of Jerusalem to hunt for a newborn King of the Jews. Herod heard about their search and was frightened by the prospect that another claimant to the throne (in this case the Messiah Himself) had risen to contest his rule over the Jews. Jerusalem also was troubled because her inhabitants knew the length to which Herod's rage and despotism could go in trying to maintain absolute control over his kingdom. Herod, as an Idumean and an outsider to Judaism, did not know the Old Testament prophecies concerning the Messiah; and so he called together all the chief priests and scribes to inquire of them where the Messiah was to be born. What is involved here is the calling of the Sanhedrin, or council of the Jews, for an official, authoritative answer. They replied, "Bethlehem of Judea," which distinguished it from Bethlehem in Galilee (Josh. 19:15).

Clearly the leaders of the Jews, including the official interpreters of the Old Testament, considered the Messiah to refer to an individual rather than the Jewish nation as a whole; and they recognized the validity of the specific prophecy of Micah 5:2 as to the place of Messiah's birth. Lenski cogently observed: "Every Jew down to this day is faced by Micah 5:2 and the Sanhedrin's answer to Herod. The Messiah is an individual not the Jewish nation itself. His birth must occur in Bethlehem and nowhere else. If Jesus is not this Messiah, then let the Jew tell us what Micah 5:2 means and let him contradict both this prophet and his own Sanhedrin if he will" (p. 63).

Though Bethlehem was a relatively insignificant place in Judea, it would be lifted to a town of first rank because from it would "come a governor who shall shepherd (or rule) my people Israel." Shepherding involves guiding, guarding, and feeding. Jesus often is referred to as a shepherd in Scripture (e.g., John 10:3-4,11; 1 Peter 2:25; 5:4). Quite in line with the conclusion of Jewish leaders who responded to Herod, the ancient rabbis believed that Micah's prophecy referred to the Messiah.

Herod proceeded to track down the Babe he viewed as a threat to his throne. From the Sanhedrin he learned the place of birth. Next he took the Magi aside privately, or "secretly" (lest people become suspicious regarding his interest), to discover when the Infant was born. If he was going to destroy the Child, it was important to discover His age.

Herod said nothing about the Infant but asked only about the star to try to pinpoint exactly when it first appeared and thus when the Child was born. Learning place and time were not enough; Herod needed to find the Baby. But of course he could not go in person to look or to send an emissary. So he sent the Magi with an urging to find the Child and report back to him so he could also worship Him.

After the audience with Herod, the Magi left promptly for Bethlehem, about two hours away. They traveled alone, without an aide from Herod's court. Though the road was easy to follow, the star which had first appeared to them in the East (and evidently had not been seen since) reappeared and "kept going before them" until it came to the very house where the holy family was living and then hovered over it. When the Magi saw the star, their "joy knew no bounds." No doubt the arrival of the Magi in Bethlehem occurred several weeks after Jesus' birth. By then there was room not only in the inn but in many other places as well. Joseph had been able to move his little family into better quarters. The shepherds of Christmas night had long since come and gone. Modern manger scenes that place shepherds and wise men together are totally inaccurate.

On entering the house, the Magi caught sight of the Babe and His mother and "fell down and worshiped Him." This was not merely obeisance to a civil ruler but homage to God because next they "offered" gifts. The word for "offered" appears only seven times in the New Testament and each time in connection with offerings to God. The gifts of gold, frankincense (an aromatic used in sacrificial offerings), and myrrh (used in perfuming ointments) indicate the affluence of the offerers.

All sorts of theories have been spun out about the symbolism of the gifts and the persons of the givers, but they are pure supposition and are best left unmentioned. As noted above, one must not conclude that these men were kings, and the fact that they brought three kinds of gifts does not necessarily mean that there were three of them. In fact, given the dangers of travel with goods of value in the ancient Middle East, it seems foolhardy for only three of them to have set out on such a journey. There is of course no question of their devotion. And there is no question of the importance of these valuable gifts to a poor, young family about to be forced into exile in Egypt and faced with subsequent expense of settlement in Nazareth. The gifts help to explain how the economic difficulties of those months were overcome.

Herod was denied the specific information on how he could get his hands on Jesus. God, who superintended the journey of the Magi from the beginning, warned them not to return to Herod; so they took another road home. Evidently they took the road going in a northeasterly direction to Jericho, crossed the Jordan, and returned home.

2. *Escape to Egypt* (2:13-15). It is impossible to be dogmatic about the sequence of events in the narrative, but it appears that the Magi had had an audience with Herod, traveled to Bethlehem, and worshiped the Christ-Child all in one day. Then they went off to find lodging for the night and received the revelation in a dream about not returning to Herod; presumably they started for home early the next morning.

Apparently about the same time that God was warning the Magi, He sent His angel to warn Joseph in a dream. From the instruction "Get up, take the child and his mother," one may conclude that Joseph was to leave for Egypt in the middle of the night or at least very early in the morning. It is clear from verse 14 that Joseph so interpreted the instruction. It would have been light enough to travel by four o'clock or earlier, depending on the time of the year. Traveling in the middle of the night was not only difficult because there were no lights, but it was also dangerous. Perhaps God provided a bright moon to light their path, and He certainly was capable of protecting them from attack.

It was more important for Joseph to hurry than it was for the Magi because Jesus was the target of Herod's murderous intent and because it was necessary to cross a lot of Herod's territory to the south before reaching the Egyptian border. The Magi were not under any direct and immediate threat of Herod, and they could more quickly get beyond his borders in the east; yet speed and secrecy were essential.

Joseph would have found it comparatively easy to settle in Egypt because hundreds of thousands of Jews already lived there. He also would be under another political administration—well beyond the long arm of Herod. Joseph was to remain in Egypt until further divine instruction. As a matter of fact, the holy family remained in Egypt until the death of Herod—probably only a few months. Then Matthew adds that this stay in Egypt was to be connected with fulfillment of prophecy. The reference is to Hosea 11:1, which states a historical fact and therefore must be a typical prophecy. That is, the historical event of Israel's childhood in Egypt is viewed as a prophetic type of Jesus' childhood in Egypt. "What was spoken by the Lord through the prophet" is another claim to inspiration, for what was spoken and we now possess in writing in Scripture is viewed as the very word of God.

3. *Slaughter of the innocents* (2:16-18). Herod anxiously awaited the return of the Magi—for one, two, or perhaps three days. Finally he realized he had been "outwitted." "Maddened with anger," he decided to rid himself of this claimant to the throne by violent measures. So he issued an order to kill all the boys in Bethlehem and its vicinity from two years old and under. Calculating on the basis of information learned from the Magi, he set the limit high enough to be sure to include Jesus.

The prophecy alluded to in verse 18 is found in Jeremiah 31:15, where it specifically referred to the Babylonian captivity. In Matthew 2:18 Rachel is viewed as the mother of Israel, sympathetic to her children's misfortunes, and is represented as rising from the tomb and uttering a double lament for the loss of her children—first by captivity and now by massacre. The inner cause of the two events is the same—Israel's sin.

4. *Return to Nazareth* (2:19-23). At length Herod died. Matthew's terse observation of the fact makes no reference to Herod's horrible end. Josephus described Herod's intestinal ulcers, the terrible convulsions he suffered in all parts of his body, and the putrification of his privy member *(Antiquities* XVII, vi. 5).

The supernatural supervision of events connected with Jesus' earthly life once more becomes evident. An angel of the Lord appeared to Joseph in a dream a second time (as promised in 2:13) and gave him his marching orders. This time the command came without urgency; there was no need for speed. And the destination was general: "the land of Israel." Evidently Joseph planned to return to Bethlehem to rear Jesus there. But when he got back into Judea, Joseph learned that Archelaus ruled there; and Joseph was afraid to stay. Actually the situation in Palestine was this. Herod had left behind three sons, and the emperor Augustus was not sure that Archelaus, Herod's choice, was capable of ruling all the domains of Herod the Great. So Augustus made him an ethnarch and put him in charge of Judea, Samaria, and Idumea. A cruel tyrant, Archelaus won the undying opposition of the Jews; and after ten years of rule, they got him exiled to Gaul for the rest of his life. A second of Herod's sons, Herod Antipas, ruled over Galilee and Perea (area east of the Jordan). A third son, Herod Philip, was granted the area northeast of the Sea of Galilee.

Plagued by his fears and in a quandary about what to do next, Joseph again received divine communication—to go to Galilee. So God led step by step: to the land of Israel, to Galilee, and then to a specific town in Galilee. God apparently did not specify that town, but Joseph followed his natural inclinations and the opportunities open to him. This too was part of God's leading ("The steps of a good man are ordered by the Lord," Ps. 37:23). It is human to want a panorama of God's plan for one's life laid out before him, but God normally leads day by day and step by step.

Once the environs of Jerusalem, a desirable place to bring up the Messiah, were no longer accessible to Joseph, it was only natural for him to return to the place he knew best. Mary had come from Nazareth (Luke 1:26), and Joseph probably also came from either the town or its vicinity. In Matthew 13:55 Joseph is called a *tektōn*, a word which always means a carpenter, but only one who makes furniture and house fittings. He was not a house builder; in Palestine houses generally were constructed of stone.

Since the family had settled in Nazareth, Jesus would be called a Nazarene, an inhabitant of Nazareth. This too was construed as a fulfillment of prophecy. There is no specific prophecy that seems to fit this fulfillment. Some have connected Jesus' growing up in Nazareth with the prophecy of Isaiah 11:1, Christ the Branch (*nēser*), involving certainly a play on words. Others have pointed to Nazareth as a small despised place, as an unlikely place for a Messiah to grow up, and thus a fulfillment of those prophecies which indicate that Messiah would be despised (Ps. 22:6; Isa. 49:7; 53:3; Dan. 9:26; cf. John 1:46; 7:52).

For Further Study

1. Compare the introductory sections of the four Gospels. Try to discover some reasons for the differences in approach in the light of the differing purpose of each writer.

2. Read two good discussions of the virgin birth in Bible dictionaries or Bible encyclopedias.

3. What do these same reference works have to say about the Magi?

4. Read either a brief or full-length biography of Herod the Great. In addition to the concise accounts in Bible dictionaries, Bible encyclopedias, and secular encyclopedias, comments by the first-century historian Josephus are interesting (see Index of Josephus).

Chapter 2

Preparation for the Messiah's Ministry
(Matthew 3:1–4:11)

A. Ministry of John the Baptist (3:1-12)

"In those days," while Jesus was residing at Nazareth, John the Baptist launched his ministry. More precisely, according to Luke 3:1, John began his preaching in the fifteenth year of the reign of the emperor Tiberius Caesar (A.D. 14-37). John commonly was known as "the Baptist," in biblical or nonbiblical sources. Even Josephus called him by that name. Though he was distinguished by his activity of baptizing, John's real work was "preaching," literally acting as a herald, announcing what his superior wanted him to announce. As Eastern royalty had heralds to precede them to announce their coming, so the Messiah had a herald to precede Him. The place of John's ministry was the northern part of the "wilderness of Judea," an area between Jerusalem and the Jordan River. Though largely uninhabited, it was not necessarily everywhere desert; for shepherds and their flocks ranged over the area, living from its meager resources.

John's message was "Repent, for the kingdom of heaven is at hand." The Greek word translated "repent" means a change of mind and involves a complete and life-changing about-face in one's attitude toward God, one's sin, and the means of salvation. One of the best illustrations of what is involved appears in 1 Thessalonians 1:9, turning (the same Greek word as in Matt. 3:2) to God from idols and serving the living God, a revolutionary change in one's life as he turns from paganism to the true God. Repentance is not an emotional state of being sorry for one's sins, though an emotional experience may accompany repentance.

"The kingdom of heaven" (literally "kingdom of the heavens") "is at hand," or "has come near," is about to come on the earth. The kingdom of heaven is so-called "because its origin, its end, its king, the character and destiny of its subjects, its laws, institutions, and privileges—all are heavenly" (Vincent, p. 24). The kingdom will of course be ruled over by the Messiah; and participation in the kingdom is based on faith in Jesus Christ and a right relationship with God, hence the need for repentance.

John's ministry was not unanticipated, for "this is he who was spoken of through the prophet Isaiah" (NIV). Again divine inspiration is claimed; the One who had spoken about John through the words of the prophet (an instrument in the hand of God), some 700 years earlier, was none other than God Himself. The prophecy of Isaiah 40:3-5 is related to John the Baptist in all four Gospels (Mark 1:2-3; Luke 3:4-6; John 1:23; and here in Matthew).

"The voice of one shouting in the wilderness": John's shouts sound like the trumpet blasts of a herald as he exhorts people to "prepare the way for the Lord." The preparation for the coming of this great Potentate, as more specifically spelled out in Isaiah 40:4, is not material but spiritual. The road for His coming will be smoothed out and obstructions removed as people repent and open their hearts for the Messiah's entrance with His forgiveness and blessing.

This one who preached in the wilderness lived as a true son of the wilderness, sharing the austerity of his surroundings. His long, loose, coarse garment was woven of camel's hair and tied around the waist with a leather belt. The belt not only kept the robe from flapping but also provided a way to tuck up the lower part of it when work or rapid movement so required. The lack of reference to sandals implies that John wore none. His clothing was the customary dress of a prophet and his appearance reminded one of Elijah, his prototype (see Mark 9:11-12; Luke 1:17; 2 Kings 1:8). Locusts were considered "clean" food according to Levitical law (Lev. 11:22) and honey was abundant in Palestine, especially in the wilder regions.

People "kept going out" (literal Greek) to John from the captital, Jerusalem, the rural areas of Judea, and the area beyond the Jordan. And Matthew might have added Galilee, from which some of his earliest disciples came (cf. John 1:35-51). One must ask why this constant parade of people endured the inconveniences of the Judean wilderness to listen to a rustic preacher with no great education or social status or other worldly attractions. Several answers may be given. First, the power of God was upon John, guaranteeing the success of his ministry (see Luke

1:14-16). Second, he preached a coming Messiah, and the messianic expectation was very much alive in Israel in those days. Third, evidently he had a high degree of personal magnetism or charisma. Fourth, John's degree of success for these or other reasons attracted the curious who also wanted to see this one who had become such a sensation.

"Confessing their sins," people "were being baptized by him in the Jordan River." Confession of sin was accompanied by baptism to indicate the acceptance of John's message. Baptism was not new in Israel. It was practiced by Jews when making proselytes, and even the members of the Qumran community engaged in ritualistic baptisms. But the significance John attached to it was new—as an outward sign of purification and life-giving change.

In verses 7-10 John stopped to warn some unwelcome guests. "Many" Pharisees and Sadducees had come to observe John's ministry. The Pharisees were fastidious in keeping the law, upheld a supernatural approach to religion, and dominated the synagogues. The Sadducees were generally antisupernatural, were politically oriented, and dominated the affairs of the temple in Jerusalem. No doubt they had come out of curiosity and also because of a degree of worry over what would happen to their position in Judaism if John became too popular. Certainly they had not come because of repentance as the others had.

"You brood of vipers" seems to be a severe form of address, but it must be attached to the following statement about fleeing from coming wrath. Bruce comments: "The serpents of all sorts lurking in the fields flee when the stubble is set on fire in harvest in preparation for winter sowing. The Baptist likens the Pharisees and Sadducees to these serpents fleeing for their lives" (p. 82). Then he encouraged them to repentance, for the coming of the Messiah and the kingdom would bring judgment. Jews believed in judgment for the heathen, but John made it clear that judgment would also fall on the godless in Israel. Having Abraham as their national ancestor would not protect them against judgment; "the Jewish nation possessed no more privilege in the eyes of God by reason of descent from Abraham than did the stones" (Atkinson, p. 776), i.e., pebbles lying at the edge of the Jordan. "The ax is already at the root of the trees," the woodsman is about to appear in judgment to cut down unfruitful trees; time for repentance is short.

In verses 11 and 12 John defines his relation to the Messiah. As may be learned from such passages as Luke 3:15-18, on this occasion some were beginning to entertain the idea that John was the Messiah. John made it clear that he was not the Messiah and that his work was only preparatory to the coming of the Messiah. In fact, John did not even consider himself worthy to carry Messiah's sandals—a slave's duty. This Coming One was mighty and powerful; "He will baptize you with the Holy Spirit [wind] and with fire," "sweeping away and consuming the impenitent, leaving behind only the righteous" (Bruce, p. 84). Verse 12 continues the thought of verse 11. This powerful One has His winnowing fork of judgment in His hand. With it He will toss up harvested wheat or barley so the wind may blow away the chaff. Then He will gather the grain into His granary and collect the chaff which has blown to one side and burn it. The passage is one of judgment in which believers and unbelievers are separated, the former going into heaven and the latter into "unquenchable fire." Unbelievers will not be consumed or annihilated in a fire that will burn itself out but will suffer eternal punishment.

B. Baptism of the Messiah (3:13-17)

"Then," at the height of John's ministry, when Jesus was about thirty years of age (Luke 3:23), He made the journey from Galilee to John specifically for the purpose of being baptized (Matt. 3:13). Where John was baptizing at the time is not certain, but probably it was near Jericho. Later he carried on his baptismal activity much farther north, at Aenon near Salim (John 3:23), not far from Bethshan, about a day's journey from Nazareth. Evidently Jesus' baptism occurred near the end of a day, after all the other candidates for baptism had been cared for (Luke 3:21).

With a repeated remonstrance (Greek tense) John tried to deter Jesus, insisting that he needed to be baptized by Jesus. John's approach implies the sinlessness of Jesus (for He had no need to repent), the sinfulness of John (as he puts himself on the level of those who came to him), and the superiority of Jesus' office and ministry to his own exalted commission.

Jesus urges, "Permit it now; for thus it is proper for us to fulfill all righteousness" (Lenski, p. 124). He does not argue with John about the convictions he has just uttered, but He says to allow it as a special case. At that moment it was proper; it had special significance in terms of fulfilling righteousness. "For us"—the offices of both were joined in fulfilling righteousness, John in requiring righteousness and Jesus in providing righteousness by His substitutionary work.

Only the fact of the baptism of Jesus is reported, not the mode or the details of procedure. No doubt God wanted it that way. As Jesus left the water He was praying (Luke 3:21). Probably as He stood on the riverbank, almost immediately thereafter the heavens opened and Jesus saw the Holy Spirit descending in a bodily form as a dove and coming upon Him (Matt. 3:16; Luke 3:22). John the Baptist also saw this divine manifestation, which to him was a sign of the messiahship of Jesus (John 1:32-33). The Spirit did not return to heaven but remained on Jesus (John 1:33), providing enablement throughout the rest of His ministry (Luke 4:18; Acts 10:38).

As the heavens opened, first the Holy Spirit made His appearance in a bodily form; then the Father spoke, "This is my beloved Son, in whom I am well pleased." Three times in Christ's ministry the Father spoke: at Jesus' baptism, at His transfiguration (17:5), and just prior to the Cross (John 12:28). The Father's statement of sonship was a testimonial to a fact; it was not a declaration that Christ was now in some sense being adopted by deity, as has been alleged. "In whom I am well pleased" is the equivalent of "in whom my pleasure rests, i.e., on whom my plan for the salvation of mankind is centered" (Tasker, p. 51).

Several truths may be gleaned from the divine response to the baptism (vv. 16-17): (1) the deity of Jesus is declared; (2) all three members of the Trinity are represented; (3) both the Father and the Spirit put their stamp of approval on the Son's part in the plan of salvation; (4) the witness of the Father and the Spirit has value for John—in convincing him of the messiahship of Jesus, and for Jesus—in encouraging Him as He entered on His atoning work and in providing the Holy Spirit's support for His human nature.

C. Temptation of the Messiah (4:1-11)

"Then," evidently immediately after the baptism, as is confirmed by comparison with Mark 1:12 and Luke 4:1, Jesus endured the temptation. Since Jesus had identified Himself with sinners and was taking upon Himself the task of redeeming them from their sins, it was to be expected that the enemy of our souls would try to block His efforts. As the prince of this world, the devil would not easily give up his subjects. If he could tempt Jesus to sin, he would destroy the whole plan of salvation; a sinful Messiah could hardly redeem fallen humanity.

But the temptation was also part of the divine plan and had divine impetus; the Spirit "led" Jesus ("drove," Mark 1:12). Among other things, the temptation would help to teach Jesus obedience (see Heb. 5:8), an obedience to be climaxed in His death on the Cross. None of us will ever understand the divine-human person of Christ, but evidently the human nature had to learn obedience. Even in the Garden of Gethsemane He prayed for the cup of suffering to be taken from Him but committed Himself to do the will of the Father (see Matt. 26:39,42).

Jesus was "led up into the wilderness." This is a literal, geographical reference, for the wilderness lies at a higher elevation than the bed of the Jordan River. Evidently the wilderness is the Judean wilderness and more specifically the largely barren region northwest of the Dead Sea. The temptation apparently continued throughout the forty days in the wilderness, as the durative construction in Mark 1:13 and Luke 4:12 implies. Jesus ate *nothing* during those days (Luke 4:2), presumably not because He was fasting but because His energies and attention were completely consumed by the constant testing of the devil. As a climax to this long period of temptation came the conversation of Matthew 4:3-10. Possibly the earlier temptations came by means of fallen angels, and, as a climax to the whole episode, Satan himself entered the picture.

As the full force of hunger descended on Jesus, Satan tried to take advantage of the situation. It is not necessary to conclude that the devil was casting doubt on Jesus' sonship in verse 3. One could just as easily interpret that as the Son of God He had no need to suffer the pangs of hunger. He could even turn some of the stones at His feet into bread. By accepting any suggestion of Satan, Jesus would in some sense be obligating Himself to Satan. But more importantly, Jesus would be trying to escape suffering that was brought on in the course of doing the Father's will.

Jesus responds by quoting Deuteronomy 8:3: "Man does not live on bread alone but on every word that comes from the mouth of God" (Matt. 3:4 NIV). He answers as the true Son of God, insisting that complete trust in the wisdom and plan of the Father was more important than satisfying immediate personal needs. The question is not what He is able to do but rather what it is His duty to do.

Next the devil took Jesus to the pinnacle of the temple in Jerusalem, a spot variously located by commentators but probably a high point on the east wall of the temple where there was a sheer drop of 500 to 600 feet into the Kidron Valley. This time the devil quoted Scripture (Ps. 91:11-12), but he did so inaccurately. Perhaps this encouragement to seek angelic care was a temptation for Jesus to "obtain more definite proof of His Father's protection by creating a situation in which He would be forced to come to the aid of His Son" (Tasker, p. 53). Again Jesus responds by quoting Scripture: "You shall not tempt the Lord your God" (Matt. 4:7; cf. Deut. 6:16). The background of Jesus' quote is found in Exodus 17, where the people demanded from God a miraculous supply of water and in so doing were in effect tempting "the Lord, saying, Is the Lord among us, or not?" (Exod. 17:7). Satan's appeal for miraculous power was analagous to Israel's demand for a miracle in the wilderness.

In the third temptation Satan moves from an attempt to persuade Jesus to prove that He is God to a direct assertion of his own deity. Satan accepts Jesus as the Messiah and acknowledges the fact of His ultimate rule over the kingdoms of this world (Rev. 11:15). But what Satan does in effect is to offer Him a way to achieve this glory without the agony of the cross. Succumbing to such a temptation would wreck the whole plan of salvation and would leave human beings trapped in the clutches of sin without hope of rescue.

Where this very high mountain was is a matter of conjecture. Certainly the traditional Mount of Temptation near Jericho was not high enough to view all the kingdoms of the world from its summit. Neither was Mount Hermon—or any other mountain for that matter. The way in which this viewing was done was clearly supernatural and beyond our understanding. But the offer of Satan was legitimate, for he is in control of the kingdoms of this world (see 2 Cor. 4:4; Eph. 2:2). Not only does Scripture attest that fact, but Jesus did not contest it. And if Satan's offer was not bona fide, this was no temptation at all. "If You fall down and worship me" refers to the kind of prostration an oriental would perform before a king and especially before a god. In the aorist tense in the Greek, this construction indicates a single act of worship, one which would elevate Satan and destroy Jesus.

A third time Jesus responds with a quotation from Scripture (Deut. 6:13). "Worship" and "serve"—the one involves the other. "Alone"— God does not share His glory with another. This time Jesus adds a word of His own: "Begone Satan!" The climax of Satan's threats has been reached. The ordeal is over for the moment. The devil left Him, but as Luke notes, only "for a season" (Luke 4:13). Jesus would again have to struggle with at least the temptation of shrinking from the agony of the Cross (Matt. 16:22-23; John 6:15; Matt. 26:39,42). As Satan left, "the angels came and continued to wait upon Him" (Williams' translation shows the force of the original). No doubt they brought food and sought to aid in His recuperation in various other ways. Matthew evidently presents the temptations in their historical order, for at the end of the third Jesus commands Satan to leave. Luke follows a geographically climactic order: desert, mountain, Jerusalem and the temple.

Before leaving the subject of Jesus' temptation, some general observations should be made about its significance. From the supernatural perspective, as noted above, it was part of the plan of God for Him; and it was part of Satan's effort to block God's provision of salvation. From the human side, it is important to our view of His priesthood and of our basis for meeting temptation. As our high priest, He does not deal with the problems of our sinful existence with detached reserve because He has *experienced* temptation in the variety of categories in which we experience it (Heb. 4:15). As we face temptation we may meet it head on as He did in His humanity by recourse to the Word of God. But of course we cannot benefit from this weapon if we do not know the Word and do not memorize important segments of it.

For Further Study

1. With the help of a concordance find all the Scripture references to John the Baptist and list the important things said about him.

2. Using some imagination, write a newspaper account of John's preaching in the wilderness.

3. What special significance might Jesus' baptism have for Him?

4. What lessons may a believer glean from Jesus' temptation that will help in meeting temptation today?

PART TWO: *Messiah's Ministry in Galilee*

Chapter 3

Beginning of the Messiah's Ministry in Galilee
(Matthew 4:12-25)

A. The Unfolding of Prophecy (4:12-17)

Matthew was not concerned with writing a chronological biography of Jesus Christ. Rather, he selected aspects of His life that picture Him as the Messiah. At this juncture (v. 12) he introduces a summary of Jesus' ministry in Galilee, when it was at its height. In so doing he skips over Jesus' winning of His first six disciples (John 1:35-51), His first miracle in Cana (John 2:1-12), His entire early Judean ministry (about a year in duration), His return to Galilee through Samaria (John 4), His seclusion in Galilee, and His journey to Jerusalem for a feast (probably the Passover, John 5).

While Jesus was in Jerusalem for that feast, word came of John's imprisonment—in the area of Perea, east of the Jordan River. Then Jesus "withdrew into Galilee." Clearly this was not for fear because Herod Antipas controlled both Perea, where he had taken action against John, and Galilee, where Jesus now retired. Perhaps He actually would have been safer in Judea (ruled by a Roman prefect), out of Herod's reach. But Jesus did not want to build too rapidly toward the culminating events of His earthly life. He had other things to do first—calling and training disciples and carrying on a fruitful ministry in Galilee.

Matthew next reported Jesus' removal of His headquarters from Nazareth (because of His rejection there, Luke 4:16-31) to Capernaum. "By the sea" points up the more strategic location of Capernaum, with access to the many other villages around the Sea of Galilee, as well as its position on the main trade route from the Mediterranean to Damascus and points East. Jesus Himself often traveled across the Sea of Galilee during His ministry. The old tribal divisions of "Zebulun and Naphtali" had long since disappeared; they were now part of Galilee and could be easily evangelized from Capernaum.

In verses 14-16 Matthew again refers to fulfillment of prophecy, this time as recorded in Isaiah 9:1-7. "Spoken through Isaiah" implies that God is the speaker and Isaiah is His mouthpiece. The background of the prophecy in Isaiah 8 is a prediction of Assyrian invasion of the northern part of Israel and its destruction in Isaiah's day. But that sentence of doom is accompanied by a promise of new hope through a descendant of David who would bring in a reign of peace. The three parts of verse 15 may be viewed as synonymous: Zebulun and Naphtali as the old Hebrew tribal divisions; "by the way of the sea" (area along the Mediterranean) and "beyond Jordan" (evidently west of the Jordan as viewed from an Assyrian perspective) as geographical areas; and "Galilee of the Gentiles" as an ethnic or political entity.

"Galilee of the Gentiles" reminds us that this region was heavily influenced by heathen elements. "The people," still Jews though corrupted, sitting in spiritual darkness, have seen the "great light" of messianic salvation brought by Jesus Christ. In the pattern of Hebrew poetic parallelism, the last half of verse 16 repeats the first half with variation.

Verse 17 serves as a general summary of Jesus' preaching. It must be connected with verse 23 and other pertinent passages to get a fuller perspective on His ministry. The description of what He said is almost identical to that of John's preaching (3:2). There is a considerable difference, however, for John's work was preparatory to Jesus' coming. With Jesus the kingdom had become a present reality. "From then on" marks the effective beginning of His ministry. With John in prison, the work of the forerunner is complete; and the One to whom he had pointed is about to step into center stage.

B. Call of Four Disciples (4:18-22)

As Jesus launched His ministry, He needed helpers. What was more natural than to call to a life of constant companionship and discipleship those who were already in some sense committed to Him. One must not make the mistake of thinking that Jesus first met these men on this occasion, won them to Himself, and then called them to a life of discipleship. Such was not the case. Simon and Andrew had been followers of John the Baptist (John 1:35-42). John had pointed them to Christ, and they had followed Him for an extended period in the previous year. Moreover, they had been present at the first miracle (John 2:2) and had been with the Master for many weeks before returning to their fishing business. James and John were partners with Simon and Andrew and therefore would have had opportunity to learn about Jesus. Furthermore, a comparison of Mark 15:40 and John 19:25 has led many to the conclusion that the mother of James and John, Salome, was the sister of the Virgin Mary; therefore James and John would have been cousins of Jesus. In His omniscience Jesus knew that these men were ready to respond to a call of apprenticeship—through which He would lead them until they became prepared and trained leaders of the church.

The call came by the Sea of Galilee, a body of water about thirteen miles long and seven miles wide, in the northern part of the Jordan River system. Apparently the more specific location was the environs of Capernaum, where these four lived and where Jesus had set up His headquarters. The call was couched in terms they would understand: "Follow me, and I will make you fishers of men." As they had caught fish and had brought them to shore for human use, so now by means of the gospel net they were to bring men to Christ for His use. Their positive response was immediate, as is clear from Mark 1:20. James and John left their fishing business and equipment in the hands of their father, Zebedee. Possibly Zebedee also took responsibility for the other half of the partnership—that belonging to Simon and Andrew.

C. Jesus' Ministry in Galilee (4:23-25)

These verses summarize Jesus' Galilean ministry, which is described more fully in later chapters. "Jesus kept going about in all Galilee," not ministering in one place as John had done. But His ministry concentrated almost entirely on the people of Israel. He taught in their synagogues, as qualified visitors sometimes were invited to do (e.g., Luke 4:16-30). And He preached the good news (gospel) of the kingdom, no doubt the good tidings that the Messiah-King had arrived to set up His kingdom. If they wished to enter the kingdom, they would have to render obedience to Him—to receive His person and His message. He healed "every disease and sickness among the people"— the miraculous works accrediting His message and messiahship.

News about Jesus spread "throughout all Syria." Syria is a general term including the whole of Palestine: Syria proper to the northeast, and Lebanon to the northwest. Actually the places mentioned in verse 25 are part of greater Syria. "Decapolis" was a league of Greco-Roman cities (originally ten in number) located mostly to the south and east of the Sea of Galilee, though one of them was on the west bank of the Jordan. "Beyond the Jordan" was the region of Perea, now the western part of the kingdom of Jordan. A quick glance at this list will show that all Palestine came under the sway of Jesus' teaching at the height of His Galilean ministry. He healed all kinds of illnesses—even the most acute forms of physical and mental derangement. Nothing was too hard for Him. Verse 24 clearly distinguishes between demon possession and ordinary physical disease.

For Further Study

1. In Bible dictionaries, encyclopedias, or geographies, study the size, terrain, and nature of Galilee.

2. From the same sources become familiar with the political geography of Palestine in Jesus' day.

3. Study the first four chapters of John to become familiar with events Matthew chose to omit from his Gospel.

Chapter 4

Principles of the Messiah's Kingdom
(Matthew 5:1–7:29)

In line with Matthew's purpose of presenting Jesus as the Messiah, he next sets forth the moral principles characterizing the kingdom Jesus proclaimed. Coming as it does after the choosing of four fishermen, this discourse appears to belong early in the Galilean ministry; but clearly Jesus delivered it at the height of His Galilean ministry after the Twelve had been chosen (see Luke 6:20-49). Even a cursory reading of the Gospels will show that Matthew's approach is topical or thematic rather than chronological. Matthew's arrangement first presents the main principles of Christ's teaching (chaps. 5–7), which sound the keynote of the new age, and then shows how they were rejected (chaps. 8–12).

Matthew 5–7 is commonly called the Sermon on the Mount because the message was delivered on a mountainside (5:1). Though one cannot be sure of the exact location, the traditional site of the Sermon is a beautiful hill overlooking the western shore of the Sea of Galilee, not far from Capernaum. The Italian Franciscan sisters maintain the Hospice and Church of the Beatitudes there.

The Sermon on the Mount has given rise to a variety of interpretations. Some, of the social gospel orientation, have concluded that here are the basic principles for the reordering of society and bringing the kingdom of God to earth. But two world wars, a nuclear arms race, and many other tragedies of recent history have shown that a universal kingdom of peace is not about to be established by human effort. This view has been almost completely discarded.

At the opposite extreme are those who believe the Sermon on the Mount has nothing to do with modern Christians. Jesus presented the kingdom and Himself as King. And, they say, since Jesus was rejected and did not establish His kingdom, the principles of the kingdom are being held in abeyance until the Lord returns to set up His kingdom. But it should be noted that the Sermon was preached to instruct men how to function while Jesus was present and after He was gone. Moreover, the principles in the Sermon also appear in the Epistles, clearly intended for the church age.

Another extreme position holds that the Sermon on the Mount presents all the basic truths of the gospel—that all that is needed for one's salvation is found in the Beatitudes, the Lord's Prayer, and the other statements Christ presents here. Such a view reduces salvation to human effort and is at variance with the clear teaching of the New Testament that salvation is by grace through faith. Moreover, it ignores the purpose of the Sermon on the Mount, which is not to present the way of salvation but principles of character and conduct for those who are members of the kingdom—who already belong to Christ.

A proper understanding of the Sermon on the Mount requires attention to its setting. Matthew wrote especially for Jews to whom Jesus presented Himself as Messiah. But the Jews had a false, materialistic concept of the kingdom and thought of the Messiah primarily as one who would bring deliverance from the Romans. Jesus set out to show them the importance of the spiritual and moral aspects of the kingdom—to demonstrate that primarily the kingdom was "within you" and that membership in it would impart a certain mind set. Rejection of the King and delay of the coming of His kingdom do not eliminate the relevance of the Sermon for contemporary Christians, who have given their allegiance to the King. As Walvoord observes, "the principles of the kingdom are far more than merely rules for a future millennium"; they proceed "from the nature of God and nature of morality and spiritual truth" (p. 45).

A. The Beatitudes (5:1-12)

Delivered to the disciples (v. 2), the Beatitudes clearly were intended for those who had given their allegiance to Christ. "Blessed" appears again and again to describe aspects of the believer's inner condition. As was true with the "blessed" one in Psalm 1, this individual is characterized not so much by what he does as by what he is. As Tasker properly observes, "The beatitudes . . . are descriptions . . . of the qualities . . . found in varying degrees, in the lives of those who have come under the influence of the kingly rule of God" (p. 61). In the same vein Kent comments, "They do not show a man how to be saved, but describe the characteristics manifested by one who is born again" (p. 937).

"Poor in spirit" might better be translated "spiritually destitute"; it denotes the opposite of spiritually self-sufficient. Such persons recognize that they have no power within themselves to please God but that they are utterly dependent on His grace. "The kingdom of heaven belongs to them" (Williams) because entrance into that kingdom will not come by proud self-sufficiency but only by God's mercy.

"They that mourn" display a grief too deep for concealment. Primarily in view are those who demonstrate an anguish for sin—their own and perhaps the evil in the world that is responsible for so much suffering. Brown views this beatitude as a complement to the first one—the former being an intellectual realization of spiritual poverty and the latter an emotional response to that condition (JFB, p. 26). One can then cry with Isaiah, "Woe is me! for I am undone" (6:5). Those who mourn for their sin shall be comforted; the comfort of forgiveness is available to all who confess their sin (1 John 1:9).

"Blessed are the meek." In the minds of many, meekness is equated with weakness. Christianity becomes a stumblingblock because strong, red-blooded men think that true Christianity expects them to become the doormats of society. Williams translates the word "lowly in mind"; that is, the meek are those who humble themselves before God in utter dependence on Him for forgiveness of sin, wisdom, and strength to move through a day effectively. Beck translates it as "Happy are those who are gentle"; probably he has grasped the true meaning of the word. One who recognizes his spiritual poverty and grieves over his own spiritual inadequacies is likely to be more patient and gentle in dealing with others. The example of gentleness *par excellence* (but not for the reason of His sinfulness) was Jesus Christ. How tender He could be in dealing with the children and all who came to Him in need! The Gentle One will impart gentleness to His followers.

But meekness does not imply weakness. Jesus could thunder at the hypocritical scribes and Pharisees and could overturn the tables of the moneychangers in the temple. Moses, who is described in Scripture as a meek man (Num. 12:3), had the fortitude to take on the pharaoh of Egypt and his whole court almost single-handedly and to deal forcefully with rebellious elements among the Israelites. Some things about Christianity need major rethinking. Disciples of Jesus

are never called upon to be pusillanimous. "Inherit the earth";
"When God has finally destroyed all who in their arrogance resist
His will, the meek will alone be left to *inherit the earth*" (Tasker,
p. 62). This promise will not be completely fulfilled until Christ establishes His kingdom on earth.

To "hunger and thirst after righteousness" is to have a keen appetite
for, a deep craving for, a deep passion for righteousness. Righteousness
may be viewed as virtually synonymous with justification or salvation or
as an upright life or as the establishment of righteousness in society. On
the latter view Tasker comments, "They long to see God's final triumph
over evil and His kingdom fully established" (p. 62). "They will be
completely satisfied" (Williams) originally applied to the feeding and
fattening of animals in a stall. It was also used to describe the meeting of
human need, as in the feeding of the 5000 (Matt. 14:20). "Satiated" is a
good alternate translation.

Brown argues that the first four beatitudes view the saints as
conscious of their need of salvation and the next three as having found
salvation and conducting themselves accordingly (p. 27).

"Blessed are those who show mercy," those who extend sympathy,
love, help, and especially forgiveness. The encouragement to show
mercy is pertinent to all ages and places, and it is related to our receipt of
mercy. Bruce properly observes, "This Beatitude states a self-acting law
of the moral world. The exercise of mercy tends to elicit mercy from
others—God and men" (p. 99). Those who show mercy "will be shown
mercy." The believer stands on a middle ground; he is to show mercy as
it has been shown him (see the parable of the unmerciful debtor, Matt.
18:23-35). We are to forgive one another as God has forgiven us (Eph.
4:32; Col. 3:13).

"Pure in heart" would seem, on the face of it, to refer to freedom
from contamination with sin. But Scripture everywhere indicates and
experience bears out that such a state cannot be achieved in this life. It
should be noted that in verses 7 and 9 single virtues are introduced, and
it has been argued that the same is true in verse 8. Thus Lenski, among
others, concludes that involved here is "singleness of heart, the honesty
which has no hidden motive, no selfish interest, and is open in all things"
(p. 192). Such single-minded individuals "are free from the tyranny of a
divided self, and . . . do not try to serve God and the world at the same
time" (Tasker, p. 62). Those who possess the nature of God will indeed
"see God." This can be true in a sense now, but it will be abundantly true

in the afterlife (see, for instance, Ps. 17:15; Heb. 12:14; 1 John 3:2).

"Peacemakers" are those who keep the peace, promote it, and seek to bring individuals into harmony with one another. They "will be called God's sons." Clearly these promoters of peace are not merely diplomats who move about the world trying to promote peace or leaders in a community who seek the same ends. We have never thought of an American secretary of state as meriting the title of a son of God for his peacemaking efforts. There is something special about the character of this activity. The Father as "the God of peace" (Heb. 13:20) and Christ as "the Prince of Peace" (Isa. 9:6) impart a family likeness to believers who enjoy peace with God through Christ and who have the peace of God in their hearts. Because of this family likeness they are recognized as children of God. No doubt the peacemaking of believers has at its core the ministry of beseeching individuals to be reconciled to God who has provided for them a full salvation (2 Cor. 5:19-20).

The last beatitude foretells the treatment that the persons described above can expect from the world. "Blessed are those who have allowed themselves to be persecuted." Lenski comments, "The idea is that they did not flee from it but willingly submitted to it when it came to them" (p. 194). "For being and doing right" (Williams)—the world cannot understand or appreciate the godly character of believers as portrayed in the Beatitudes; it even finds such character obnoxious. Because goodness rebukes the world's sinfulness, the world turns against them and even persecutes them. Jesus assures such persecuted ones that maltreatment for their faith and godly conduct is evidence that they are members of the kingdom of heaven.

After the Messiah leaves the scene, all sorts of evil will be heaped upon His followers "falsely." They are not to grieve or feel sorry for themselves under such conditions but are to "Keep on rejoicing and leaping for ecstasy" (Williams; cf. Acts 5:41) because of the great reward that is set before them. Moreover, "They must rejoice greatly in the knowledge that such suffering is an indication that they are in the true line of descent from the prophets who foretold the Messiah's coming" (Tasker, p. 63). Perhaps James 1:2-4, "Count it all joy when you fall into various trials" is applicable here; that is, rejoice over the opportunities that trials bring for growth and development in the Christian life.

B. The Influence of the Kingdom Citizens (5:13-16)

Believers may suffer persecution at the hands of unbelievers, but they are very important to the unbelieving world. Kingdom citizens are to function as salt and light. Salt preserves; it arrests decay or acts as an antiseptic. Thus believers are a restraint on the world's corruption. Salt flavors foods and makes them more palatable. Believers can bring a special kind of grace and pleasantness to an otherwise ugly and unhappy world. Salt induces thirst; so believers by their exemplary lives are to create a thirst among non-Christians for the higher life in Christ. And just as the human body suffers and could even die without enough salt, so the social organism suffers without enough Christians to influence it. Believers who do not live effectively before unbelievers are like salt that has lost its saltness; it is good for nothing and might as well be tossed out into the garbage.

Believers as the light of the world are to function actively in dispelling darkness. Light shows the way so a traveler may move more easily along the road; believers are to show the way to God. Light promotes life and growth; believers are to be involved in the process of encouraging spiritual growth. Light gives a proper perspective on things which often take on grotesque appearance in darkness or semidarkness. Christians have the privilege of bringing to bear a divine perspective on the affairs of man and his society. The light which Christians disseminate is not their own but derives from Christ who is Himself the Light of the World (John 8:12).

Diffusion of light has a public aspect (as a city built on a hill which illuminates lower levels) and a private or domestic aspect (put on a lampstand in a house instead of under a peck measure). The lamp to which Jesus referred was a small olive oil burning object that could be held in the palm of one's hand. The purpose of letting one's light shine in witness and acts of loving service was not to engender self-glorification but to bring honor and praise to God, the source of all light.

C. Jesus and the Mosaic Law (5:17-48)

1. *Jesus' relationship to the law* (5:17-20). To those who might be fearful that Jesus would not have proper reverence for the authority and principles of the Old Testament or who might hope that He would become a religious revolutionary, Jesus issued a categorical statement. He came not to annul or abrogate the Old Testament law in any respect but to fulfill it. He would fulfill it by keeping it perfectly, by embodying it in living form, and by "paying the full penalty of the Law as the Substitute for sinners" (Kent, p. 937).

Then comes the first recorded use of Jesus' magnificent formula: "Truly I say to you." He spoke with supreme authority; He did not need to quote another. Thus He put Himself on a level with God. Brown observes, "No higher claim to an authority *strictly divine* could be advanced. For when we observe how jealously Jehovah asserts it is His exclusive prerogative to give law to men (Lev. xviii. 1-5; xix. 37; xxvi. 1-4, 13-16, etc.), such language as this of our Lord will appear totally unsuitable, indeed abhorrent, from any creature-lips" (pp. 30-31).

"Till heaven and earth pass away" refers either to the permanence of the law or to its applicability until heaven and earth literally do pass away and a new heaven and earth come into being (cf. Matt. 24:35; Rev. 21:1). "Jot" is the smallest Hebrew letter (yodh), and "tittle" is a stroke or projection which distinguishes some Hebrew letters from others. In the statement, "Not the smallest letter or stroke will pass from the law until all is fulfilled," Jesus clearly is assuming biblical inerrancy.

Continuing to support the authority of the law, Jesus condemns "anyone who annuls [or makes invalid] one of the least of these commandments" (NASB). Reference clearly is to the Pharisees who by their systems of interpretation sometimes actually violated or twisted the intent of Scripture. But of course teachers in the church are capable of doing the same thing today. Conversely those who "practice and teach" others to respect and follow the commands of God will have an exalted position in the kingdom. The Jewish establishment, and especially the Pharisees of Jesus' day, had a great deal to say about the nature of the law, keeping the law, and establishing a standing before God based on scrupulous adherence to the law. But Jesus categorically states that unless one's righteousness surpasses that of the scribes and Pharisees, he cannot be a member of the kingdom at all. Righteousness would have to exceed that of the Pharisees in kind rather than degree; it would have to be an inner righteousness based on a proper relationship to God rather than an external show of righteousness based merely on conformity to a certain pattern of conduct.

Next Jesus proceeds to make five comparisons between aspects of the Mosaic law as commonly understood or commonly interpreted by the scribes and as interpreted in terms of the deeper spiritual principles of the kingdom.

2. *The sin of anger* (5:21-26). "You have heard that it was said to the people long ago, 'Do not murder'" (NIV). Knowledge of the law was gained by hearing it read in the synagogues, and the specific command

not to murder was a true statement of both Pharasaic interpretation and of the law itself. Reference is to the sixth commandment as stated in Exodus 20:13 and Deuteronomy 5:17. Parenthetically, it should be noted that the commandment does not say "Do not kill" but rather "Do not murder." In other words, neither war nor capital punishment are forbidden by the commandment. "Whoever murders will have to answer to the court" (Williams). "It restrained the end not the beginning of transgression" (Bruce, p. 106); and it could deal only with overt or external infringements of the law, not the roots of the crime.

Jesus proceeds to internalize the Mosaic injunction or to show that murder has its roots or its birth in anger and contempt. "I say to you" (cf. v. 18) again marks Jesus' authority as lawgiver and judge. Anger certainly has the restriction of "without a cause," though it does not appear in the best manuscripts of this passage (see Eph. 4:26). "Brother" must apply to a fellow human being. "Raca" cannot be positively translated; perhaps it means "brainless" or "emptyheaded." Certainly it is an expression of contempt. "Brainless" and "fool" sound rather tame to us and do not seem to warrant severe condemnation. But of course it is impossible to discover their full significance in first-century society. What is indicated is violent passion giving vent to some fierce name calling. Evidently three levels of punishment are intended in verse 22. Some interpret the verse to mean that persons guilty of such sins of the heart deserve to go before the courts. Others believe that when the King rules in person, He will have the omniscience to judge attitudes of the heart as effectively as overt crimes.

Verse 23 has a practical application of what has just been said. In consequence of the fact that anger and bad feelings between brethren make one liable for punishment, one should set his relationships straight. The picture is Jewish. An individual has come to the court of the Jews in the temple with an offering to God and seeking divine forgiveness. As he stands at the railing of the court of the priests waiting for his offering to be accepted and sacrificed on the altar, he remembers that he has wronged someone who now has a just complaint against him. The offerer should go and remove roadblocks to fellowship with others before he expects roadblocks to fellowship with God to be removed. This injunction has a current relevance. One cannot expect to have clear channels of fellowship with God if the channels of fellowship with others are clogged. One who is miserable in the fellowship of believers will hardly enjoy a pleasant fellowship with God.

Verses 25 and 26 present the case of a debtor and creditor on the way to court. Apparently the creditor is somewhat flexible or well-disposed because the debtor is the one who is encouraged to square accounts. These verses may be another way of describing settling accounts between a human offender and the one he has wronged, or they may be a parable alluding to the certainty of divine punishment on those who do not "square accounts" with God. If the latter is true, the last part of verse 26 cannot be made to teach that one may sometime pay his debt to God and find release from hell. Punishment after death is always described as eternal in Scripture (e.g., Matt. 25:41,46) and no human being is capable of paying a spiritual debt to God (e.g., Isa. 64:6). It should be remembered that parables have one main point to teach; we should not press them in all details.

3. *The sin of lust* (5:27-30). "You have heard it was said"; you have heard from the scribes and Pharisees who recounted the law of Moses. Reference is to the seventh commandment (Exod. 20:14; Deut. 5:18): "You shall not commit adultery." The tendency had been to treat this prohibition as a public law and to stress the overt act. As in the case of Jesus' comment on the sixth commandment, He here dwells on the immoral desire which leads to the outward act. "Anyone," either married or unmarried, "who continues to look at a woman," with a persistent desire, "to lust after her has already committed adultery with her in his heart." "Committed" is in the aorist tense, indicating an act occurring at a point in time in the past. The sin already has been committed "in his heart" and is just as much a sin as the overt act. Perhaps it should be added that Jesus' statement is just as applicable to any woman as to any man.

If an eye proves to be a "trap-spring" or "causes you to stumble," "tear it out." "The *eye* is here regarded as the medium through which temptation comes, and the *hand* as the instrument by which sin is committed" (Tasker, p. 69). As any diseased member is to be amputated that a life may be saved, so a right eye or a right hand is to be severed to preserve life spiritually.

Of course literal mutilation will accomplish nothing because a left eye and a left hand can get into just as much mischief as the right ones; and a person with no eyes and no hands can be just as sinful as one who possesses all four members. What is being said is symbolical of strenuous efforts to master temptation. One may have to cut off reading some kinds of literature, going to some kinds of places, or associating with some individuals—in short, to cut off the occasions that tend to stimulate unholy passions. A more restricted manner of life, though it may sometimes seem to be rather confining, is better than a more freewheeling existence that may lead to the destruction of one's testimony and ultimately even of his very life. This holy restraint is true Christian asceticism. Of course what really has to happen is a change of one's heart or his inner self, a regeneration or new birth, if he would escape being "thrown into hell" (NASB).

4. *Divorce* (5:31-32). The topic shifts naturally from purity in sexual relations to divorce. Views on the subject and Jewish practice at the time of Christ were very loose. Under the influence of those who followed Rabbi Hillel, almost any pretext could be used for divorcing one's wife, though a wife could not divorce her husband. Those of the school of Shammai, however, prohibited divorce for any reason except adultery. Reference here is to Deuteronomy 24:1, which is quoted in abbreviated form, alluding only to the last half of the verse concerning the necessity of certificate of divorce. Apparently this was so because the scribes concerned themselves only with the form of the bill of divorcement and did nothing about capricious husbands and the disintegration of the family.

In verse 32 Jesus came down hard on the side of the school of Shammai and acknowledged only one ground for divorce. "Causes her to commit adultery" means that a husband drives her into it in case she marries again. The last half of the verse concerns the remarriage of women who have been divorced for trivial reasons. Williams has properly translated the phrase thus: "Whoever marries a woman who is thus divorced commits adultery." The question of whether persons who are divorced from an unfaithful partner may remarry is not settled by this verse. Jesus takes up the divorce question again in Matthew 19:3-11.

5. *Oaths* (5:33-37). "Do not swear falsely" or "Do not perjure yourself" is not a direct quotation but a summary of Old Testament teaching on the subject of making oaths (see Exod. 20:7; Lev. 19:12; Num. 30:3; Deut. 23:22). In their casuistry the scribes had worked out a classification of which oaths were binding and which were not, with no real regard for the integrity of the individual or an inner truthfulness on his part. Jesus cut away all this scribal artificiality and issued a categorical command to "swear not at all."

Though the scribes had claimed that oaths which did not mention the name of God were not binding, Jesus showed that they were.

Swearing by heaven was the same as swearing by God's throne, by the earth the same as swearing by His footstool, and by Jerusalem the same as swearing by His holy city. In fact, even swearing by one's head "implicates the one who holds power over it" (Kent, p. 938). Let your communication be a simple yes or no (see James 5:12); "be as good as your word even unsupported by an oath" (Bruce, p. 111). "Anything beyond these is of evil" (NASB) may mean that the adding of oaths to our affirmations or denials may be an admission that our usual speech cannot be trusted or may be a capitulation or condescension to the level of untruthfulness in society in general. Evidently Jesus' prohibition refers to personal relationships and not to taking an oath in a court of law because He Himself took an oath before the high priest (Matt. 26:63-64).

6. *Retaliation* (5:38-42). Verse 38 is a quotation from Exodus 21:24, which spells out the law of retribution, a principle of civil law that made the punishment fit the crime and took vengeance out of the hands of a person wronged and put it in the hands of a magistrate. Jesus does not condemn this principle but "insists that a disciple should be ready to suffer loss rather than to resort to personal vindictiveness" (Tasker, p. 67). This was in line with Old Testament teaching: "Thou shalt not avenge, nor bear any grudge against the children of thy people" (Lev. 19:18).

"Do not resist evil" refers either to the evil one, a person doing evil (not Satan), or the injury being done. Personal injury is in view; this statement does not teach that evil is never to be resisted. Rather than avenging himself against one who has done him wrong, the believer is to go to the opposite extreme. Verses 39-42 drive home the point. These exhortations may seem to make Christians human doormats, but this is not necessarily so. To be sure this is not the world's way of doing things, but even on a purely rational level it is not stupid. The Book of Proverbs talks about being kind to one's enemy and thus heaping "coals of fire upon his head" (Prov. 25:22). Sometimes we speak of killing someone with kindness. By being kind to those who are nasty to us, frequently we disarm them and sometimes even transform them.

As is clear from the following verses, what are mentioned serve only as examples of categories of injury and are not necessarily to be taken literally. They drive home the point of developing the opposite of a vengeful attitude. Kent tabulates the categories of suffering as follows: "A child of God should willingly suffer loss by assault (v. 39), lawsuits (v.

40), compulsory regulations (v. 41), begging (v. 42*a*), and loans (v. 42*b*)" (pp. 938-9).

To turn the other cheek is not literally to invite further indignities but to be willing to endure them if they come. This comes clear from Jesus' own conduct before His crucifixion (John 18:22). When smitten He did not literally turn the other cheek. If anyone wants to sue you for your tunic, equivalent to a suit (in pledge for a debt, Exod. 22:26-27), let him have your overcoat (cloak) too. A cloak could not by law be retained overnight as a pledge because it was often used as a bed blanket (Exod. 22:26). "If anyone makes you go one mile" alludes to the requirement of Roman and oriental governments that citizens perform various services without remuneration. Here the reference may be to postal service or the carrying of a burden of some kind (e.g., Simon of Cyrene, Matt. 27:32). "If anyone keeps on begging you" (for a gift) or wants to borrow from you, turn not away in unfeeling refusal to relieve extreme need. This does not say, "Give him everything he asks for."

In conclusion, Lenski well observes, "Christ's injunctions are not intended to be applied mechanically . . . or with foolish blindness which loses sight of the true purposes of love. Love is not to foster crime in others or to expose our loved ones to disaster and perhaps death. . . . Christ never told me not to restrain the murderer's hand, not to check the thief and robber, not to oppose the tyrant, or by my gifts to foster shiftlessness, dishonesty, and greed" (p. 244).

7. *Love of enemies* (5:43-48). "Love your neighbor" comes from Leviticus 19:18,34 and summarizes the second table of the law (Matt. 22:39). "Hate your enemy" was an inferred corollary added by the scribes and Pharisees, who came to regard Gentiles generally as their enemies. "I say" shows the Lord of the law speaking with authority. Jesus countermands this Pharisaical addition and returns to the true spirit of the Old Testament. "Love your enemies," not with a mere affection, but with a higher kind of love *(agapē)* which "seeks to bestow true blessings upon the one loved, to do him the highest good . . . to free [his] enemy from his hate, to rescue him from his sin, and thus to save his soul" (Lenski, p. 246). Prayer for those who "persecute" must be to the end that one's enemies will be converted. The two middle clauses of the verse as found in the KJV do not appear in the best manuscripts.

This kind of love will certainly demonstrate that "you are the sons of your Father" because it has a godlike character. It is possible only through the enablement of the indwelling Holy Spirit, and resembles that of Jesus Christ while on the cross as He prayed for His executioners (Luke 23:34). Moreover, if you love your enemies, you will be like God, who provides sunshine and rain equally for the righteous and unrighteous. Verses 45 and 46 need little comment. There is no particular merit or anything extraordinary in loving those who love you. Unbelievers in general do that, and the hated tax collectors (publicans) in particular do too.

"Be perfect as your heavenly Father is perfect" has become the basis of all sorts of erroneous teaching. The subject here cannot be sinless perfectionism because that is entirely foreign to the context. Jesus has been talking about loving one's enemies and has made the point that God blesses both the righteous and unrighteous. Then comes the exhortation to be perfect or mature or complete like God, which must mean to be all-encompassing in one's demonstration of good will or kindness. Kent has well said, "The command *Be ye therefore perfect* is to be restricted to the matter of love in this context. As God's love is complete, not omitting any group, so must the child of God strive for maturity in this regard (cf. Eph. 5:1,2)" (p. 939).

D. False and True Piety (6:1-18)

Jesus contrasts the true piety He expects of children of the kingdom with the false piety or hypocrisy of the scribes and Pharisees. The one characterized by true piety is concerned primarily with relation to God and His approval rather than the applause of men. The Father as the Seeing and Knowing One is mentioned ten times in these eighteen verses. Jesus discusses the three cardinal works of Jewish religious life—almsgiving, prayer, and fasting—not to condemn them, but to urge the right motivation in performing them.

1. *Alms* (6:1-4). "Be careful not to do your 'acts of righteousness' before men, to be seen by them" (NIV). Yes, we are to let our light shine (5:16); but what we do is to promote the cause of Christ in the world, not to bring self-glorification. "To be seen by them" reveals true motivation. Though the works may be good, when the motivation is wrong, we have no reward from our Father in heaven. God abominates duplicity.

"Whenever you do alms" indicates that periodic acts of charity are expected. "Sound a trumpet" is probably to be taken metaphorically for publicizing or showing ostentation. Williams captures the contemporary colloquialism thus: "Never blow your own horn in public." But alms chests in the temple and synagogue were trumpet-shaped, and large coins dropped with force in these metal containers would "herald" the act of giving. A "hypocrite" was an actor who wore a mask in a play; so a hypocrite in Jesus' condemnation was one who played a part in life, one whose religion was external and unreal and was not a true reflection of his inner self. "They have received their reward in full" was a commercial term used for accounts receipted in full. They received what they wanted—the plaudits of men; and that is all they will get.

To give in such a way that one's left hand does not know what his right hand is doing is a figure of speech for giving with simplicity, with no display, with no dwelling on the matter even in one's own thoughts. The emphasis on "secret" in this passage does not mean that all giving must be anonymous. Rather, the issue is primarily between the donor and God, without ostentation. A member of the congregation quietly drops his check into the offering plate. The treasurer and others in the church will know about the gift. A benefactor of a college may give a new building and may present his check to the president and/or the board of trustees; subsequently his gift may be widely announced. But the giver gave quietly; he did not call an all-school convocation to make the announcement or insist that his name be on the building or that a plaque with his name grace the front hall. "Openly" should be omitted from verse 4. The Father may reward openly, privately, or ultimately in heaven—in a way that pleases Him.

2. *Prayer* (6:5-15). Jesus now turns to criticism of the ostentatious prayers of the scribes and Pharisees. Standing to pray was the usual manner of praying and is not condemned; neither is public prayer, for Jesus Himself engaged in it (Luke 10:21-22; John 11:41-42). As with almsgiving, only the wrong motive is scored: "to be seen by people." And as with almsgiving, since what they really wanted was to be noticed, "they have their reward in full."

In contrast to the Pharisees, true believers are to go into a place of retirement and shut the door and pray. They are to pray in complete privacy—"in secret," where there is no other human being to impress. "Your Father who sees in secret," in the secret place and the most secret recesses of the heart and mind, "will reward you," as for any other good work sincerely performed. "Openly" should be omitted as in verse 4. Private prayer is excellent preparation for public prayer; if one can meet God honestly and properly in the former, presumably he can in the latter.

"Do not babble like the Gentiles," who by endless repetition and many words try to tire out their gods and weary them into granting requests. Inhabitants of the fairly cosmopolitan province of Galilee would be familiar with pagan practices, and Jews themselves were not beyond carrying on in the same way. Though prayer by the yard is folly, Jesus was not condemning length or even repetition if one was agonizing before his God. Jesus Himself prayed all night and was even repetitive (Luke 6:12; Matt. 26:44).

Next Jesus gives some instruction on prayer. Frequently this is called "The Lord's Prayer," but it may better be called "The Disciples' Prayer." The Lord's Prayer appears especially in John 17 and the various passages that concern His agony in the Garden of Gethsemane (e.g., Matt. 26:39-46). What Jesus enunciates here is not a model prayer to be prayed ritual style but some principles for proper or effective prayer. (Since the context of Luke 11:1-4 is so different from the Matthew passage, this prayer is thought to have been repeated on another occasion.)

"Our Father" shows this prayer is to be offered by believers only. "Father" connotes membership in the family of God, reverential trust, fatherly watch-care of God, and a certain obligation to grant requests—but only those which are good for His children. "Hallowed be thy name" means may Your name be reverenced—and certainly not among Jews only. "Thy kingdom come" must apply in the first instance to the literal rule of God on earth in the messianic kingdom, but it may also concern "the kingdom of God within you" (cf. Luke 17:21). Thus it may be a prayer that the kingdom of God may more completely dominate our lives "and that more and more of our fellows may be brought under the saving sway of that kingdom" (Macaulay, p. 41). Certainly the will of God is done in heaven; there is no clash of wills in the presence of God. The heavenly obedience becomes a pattern for conditions on earth. Perhaps "thy will be done in earth, as it is in heaven" is an explanation of "thy kingdom come."

Petitions of the prayer shift from concerns of God to concerns of man. "Our daily bread" is a request for the supply of personal needs, for what we need to sustain bodily life. "Forgive us our debts" refers to moral debts or sins. These are the sins of believers which require frequent confession (1 John 1:9). "As we have forgiven our debtors" means those who sin against us. What is in view here and in verses 14-15 is, of course, the sin of believers. It is incongruous for a believer to ask God to forgive his sins and then refuse to forgive the sin of another against him. But what is said here appears to be a kind of legalism or forgiveness of sin on the basis of works and God's refusal to bestow His grace. On closer look, none of these is true. A believer who refuses to be reconciled to a brother is living in a state of sin; his refusal to make things right is itself a sin. And he can hardly go to God and ask forgiveness for refusal to bury grudges or in other ways to make things right. Hence as long as he refuses to forgive, he cannot expect to be forgiven. So his fellowship with God is strained; his salvation is not threatened.

"Bring us not into temptation," or "bring us not into trial." It is clear from Scripture that God does not tempt us to sin (e.g., James 1:13), but He does test or try believers. And of course Satan may take advantage of a testing. In struggling with this difficult phrase Bruce concludes, "We incline to take it as a prayer against being *drawn* or sucked, *of our own will*, into temptation" (p. 41). Somewhat similarly Williams translates this phrase as "Do not let us be subjected to temptations."

"But deliver us from evil" should be regarded as the second part of the petition just introduced. "Deliver" in the Greek aorist tense refers to rescue or deliverance from specific dangers, not continual preservation from danger. "Evil" may refer to the evil one or evil in an impersonal sense. The latter seems preferable—from all evil of whatever kind, from sin and all its consequences. The well-known doxology at the end of the prayer appears only in later Greek manuscripts and evidently does not belong to the original.

3. *Fasting* (6:16-18). Fasting often accompanied prayer. The Mosaic law required fasting on the Day of Atonement (Lev. 16:29; 23:27). In addition Jews fasted on anniversaries of national calamities and on other special occasions. The Pharisees also fasted every Thursday (the day Moses ascended Mount Sinai) and Monday (the day he came down from Sinai). These twice-weekly fasts became great displays of piety for the Pharisees who put on a "gloomy" or "sad" appearance and disfigured their faces (Beck), probably with ashes, to show they were fasting. As with prayer and almsgiving, the Pharisees sought a reputation of holiness; and as before, in so doing "they have received their payment in full."

Jesus did not institute any fasts among the disciples, but fasting was practiced in the early church. As good Jews, many Christians continued to fast after coming into the church. To such, Jesus issues the injunction to wash and dress normally so as to make no display of fasting. This spiritual exercise is to be a private matter between God and the worshiper. Again, the Father will give the proper reward or blessing. As in verses 4 and 6, "openly" is to be omitted here.

E. Worldly Wealth and Cares (6:19-34)

1. *True perspective on wealth* (6:19-24). The Pharisees in particular and Jews in general put considerable emphasis on wealth as an evidence of God's approval. And of course Jews and Gentiles of all ages commonly have sought security in material wealth rather than in a proper relationship to God and His provision. Treasures on earth, of whatever kind, are perishable. Oriental wealth often consisted in embroidered garments or fabrics, which "moths" or other insects could totally ruin. "Rust" is "a generic term embracing the whole class of agents which eat or consume valuables" (Bruce, p. 123). Almost anything we hold dear is capable of spoilage or decay (even loved ones or reputations or little empires of various sorts). Wealth in jewelry or precious metals could easily be carried off by "thieves" who may "dig through" mudbrick or stone walls rather than try to break down barred doors or windows.

The true wealth of the kingdom citizen should be stored up in heaven where it is not susceptible to decay and destruction. The primary reason why wealth in heaven will not decay is that it will be of a different character. Laying up treasures in heaven involves using all our talents, our material goods, our time, and our energies in a way well pleasing to God and beneficial to others. A life of obedience to God and service to others will bring a "recompence of the reward" (Heb. 11:26). Laying up treasure in heaven will bring dividends now and in the life to come.[1] "Where your treasure is, there will your heart be." "A man's heart inevitably follows his treasure; he is in love with what he believes to be his highest good" (Tasker, p. 75). "To have a heart in heaven means to be utterly devoted to the interests of Christ" (Atkinson, p. 781).

But what if the individual says that he has a treasure on earth and a treasure in heaven, that he has a divided affection? The following parable deals with that question. "The eye is the light of the body," the window through which light enters the body. "If the eye is single" or healthy or clear in vision, it "presents a well-defined and single image to the brain" (Alford, p. 65), and the "whole body will be full of light." The one with the eye that is "single" is "entirely devoted to the interests of Christ and the service of God" (Atkinson, p. 781).

---

[1]For an extended discussion of "laying up treasures in heaven," see D. Martyn Lloyd-Jones, II, pp. 82-85.

The one with an "evil eye" or unclear or double vision has no window through which light can come and his body is filled with darkness. If one is covetous or grudging or diseased by a false sense of values, his whole outlook is dark indeed. The last sentence of verse 23 seems to mean that if one's spiritual perception is perverted by a twisted or unclear sense of direction, then the darkness that already exists as a result of one's sinful nature becomes dark indeed.

One cannot be a slave to God and money (mammon) at the same time (heavenly and earthly treasures cannot be laid up at the same time), "for single ownership and full-time service are of the essence of slavery. The accumulation of wealth is so absorbing an occupation that sooner or later money enslaves its victims, and leads them to despise the God to whom they may have imagined they could render a limited allegiance" (Tasker, p. 76).

All this discussion on wealth does not mean that it is wrong for a Christian to make money or to amass wealth. If he has wealth, he views it as belonging to God and to be used for His glory. The believer is merely God's steward or a caretaker for God. The believer is not held in the grip of or in bondage to possessions but holds them loosely in his hand—is in a state of detachment from them.

2. *Cure for anxiety* (6:25-34). Those with wealth may become slaves to it; those without much of this world's goods may fall victims to worry about the supply of daily needs. The disciples would fit into the latter category and apparently were concerned about supply of necessities, for Jesus told them "stop worrying." The argument of verse 25 is this: God gave life and the body, will He not care for both by providing the lesser gifts of food and clothing?

In His comments about the birds, Jesus is not commending sloth, for birds are very busy building nests, gathering food, and providing for their young. The emphasis is on the fact that in God's order of nature He provides even for these lowly or insignificant creatures, and as heavenly Father He puts a far greater value on His spiritual children. Naturally He will care for the members of His spiritual family. "Who of you by worrying can add a single hour to his lifespan?" is an almost laughable question because worry only shortens life; worry can kill a person. "Lifespan" rather than "stature" is the common meaning of this word as used in the papyri.

Next Jesus turns from food to clothing. The "lilies," flowers of uncertain identity, grow wild in the fields, without human care. Yet the robes of Solomon, Israel's most ostentatious king, were never as beautiful as the blossoms of these flowers, which God Himself has endowed. These flowers are really insignificant. After a short growing season the foliage on the hillsides of Palestine dries up with the cessation of spring rains and the coming of the hot summer sun. In this fuel-starved area, dried grasses and flowering plants are then used to start fires for cooking, baking bricks, and firing pottery. Again Jesus contrasts God's care for the spring growth on the hillsides with the greater care God has for His children.

"You of little faith" may be viewed both as a rebuke and an encouragement to spiritual growth. "So do not worry"; meditation on the fatherly watch-care of God is a sure cure for worry. "All these things the Gentiles eagerly seek" (NASB) because they do not know God as heavenly Father. Therefore they fancy that they have to provide for all their material needs on their own and of course are full of anxiety when supplies grow short. You have a Father in heaven who knows your needs "even before you ask him" (v. 8). Leave all your worries to Him.

While unbelievers "seek eagerly" after material things, Jesus' followers are to "go on seeking," as their supreme pursuit, the kingdom and the righteousness of the kingdom. If spiritual concerns take precedence in our lives, we shall have a proper perspective on the supply of our material needs. Seeking "first" the kingdom implies a "second" seeking for material good and does not teach that we should then be shiftless and irresponsible in providing for our families and ourselves. It means that we shall approach the supply of "our daily bread" (6:11) with confidence in the all-powerful heavenly Father who cares for His children. Thus we shall be free from anxiety, "and all these things will be given to you as well" (NIV).

"Therefore do not worry about tomorrow." "To restrict care to to-day is to master it absolutely. It is the future that breeds anxiety and leads to hoarding" (Bruce, p. 127). "Each day has enough trouble of its own" (NIV) observes that we have enough difficulties to face and master today with God's help; there is no sense in going into the future to borrow more. Anxiety commonly develops because we imagine a set of circumstances in the future that *we cannot handle*. The truth is that we cannot look into the future with any degree of certainty. Most of what we fear about the future never comes to pass. Of course we shall worry about what we cannot handle. But children of the heavenly Father do not try to handle life on their own; they trust Him to deal with the many circumstances and challenges of life.

F. Concluding Exhortations to Kingdom Citizens (7:1-29)

1. *Judging others* (7:1-6). "Do not judge, or you too will be judged" (NIV). It is clear from the Greek of verse 1 and the context that the prohibition stated is against censoriousness rather than exercise of the critical faculty, which is of course at the basis of successful living. Self-righteous, hypocritical judging demoralizes the one attacked, increases the self-righteousness of the one who does it, and causes hard feelings and divisions in the religious group where it is practiced. Moreover, Jesus warns that it brings on retaliation in like measure (v. 2) and a certain judgment by Christ at the last day ("You will be judged").

In verses 3-5 Jesus illustrates His point with a parable. This is commonly interpreted to mean that a person with an evident major fault (with a large piece of timber in the eye) is in no position to put right an offender with some trivial defect (splinter in the eye). He should first seek to right his own major wrong before he tries to set others straight. Lenski points out, however, that the splinter and beam were located in the eyes, not in other parts of the body. Then he concludes, "Jesus is not speaking of faults or sins in general, one being tiny, the other immense, but of moral perception which is slightly wrong in the one man, totally wrong in the other. He who is devoid of all truly moral judgment pretends to aid another who is slightly wrong in his judgment" (p. 290).

In any case, one who would reprove the faults of others must first judge himself. In so doing he will become so aware of his own imperfections and his own need of forgiveness and compassion that when he is called on to judge others, he will do so with moderation and love rather than in self-righteous smugness and severity.

Verse 6 shows that though censorious judgment is to be shunned, judicious discrimination is not. "Dogs," unclean vicious scavengers in ancient Palestine, and "swine," unclean animals Jews were forbidden to raise, do not refer to Gentiles or publicans and sinners here because Jesus preached to both. Rather, reference is to individuals who have heard the gospel and have viciously scorned it. "Sacred things" and "pearls" are identical (the truths of the gospel) and should not be wasted or exposed indiscriminately to desecration or vile treatment of those who adamantly oppose them.

2. *Admonition to prayer* (7:7-12). The concluding exhortations of

the Sermon on the Mount may appear to be somewhat heterogeneous, but probably they were excerpted from a rather elongated discussion of Jesus with His disciples. This section on prayer does seem to relate closely to the preceding, however. In order to judge ourselves and to have the wisdom to carry out the command given in verse 6 we need to pray. Verses 7 and 8 each contain a triplet with an ascending climax. The force of the present imperatives in verse 7 is to encourage persistence or perseverance and frequency in prayer: keep on asking, seeking, knocking. With each petition comes a promise of divine response in verse 7 But to underscore the commitment of the heavenly Father to provide for His children, Jesus repeats and individualizes the promises in verse 8: "everyone," "one." Of course it is assumed that these prayers are offered in faith and with an honest purpose (see James 1:5-7; 4:3).

Then to emphasize further God's fatherly kindness, Jesus injects an illustration. If one of you has a son who asks for bread, who will mock him by giving him a stone (round and smooth like a Palestinian loaf)? Or if he asks for a fish, who will give him a serpent (a serpent resembles an eel), also unfit to eat? The idea of a serpent stinging is not implied because it would be dead. If an earthly father with his sinful nature will give good gifts to his children when they ask, how much more will the sinless heavenly Father give good things to those who keep on asking Him!

The so-called Golden Rule (v. 12) can easily be joined to what has been discussed above rather than treating it as a separate topic. "Therefore," "instead of judging others falsely, we shall do to them what we would that they should do to us" (Lenski, p. 295). The Golden Rule is a summary of the second table of the law (love to man). It was not necessary for Jesus to summarize the first table of the law (love to God) because He has been talking about the disciples' relation to the Father, about prayer to Him, absolute dependence on Him, and seeking first the kingdom of God and His righteousness. Thus Jesus could say, "This sums up the Law and the Prophets" (NIV).

Jesus was speaking to believers when He uttered the Golden Rule, and He certainly intimated its connection with the first table of the law. It is important to heed Lenski's warning: "Those who separate the Golden Rule from the first table and from our relation to God as our Father by faith in Christ Jesus ignore the Law and the Prophets when they claim that love to our neighbor is enough to admit us to heaven" (p. 296). The Golden Rule was never given to the world at large, and only those who are believers and have the Holy Spirit indwelling them have the power to make the Golden Rule a reality in their lives.

3. *The two gates* (7:13-23; cf. Jer. 21:8; 1 Cor. 1:18). At least by this point in the Sermon on the Mount, Jesus has more listeners than just the disciples (v. 28). He next exhorts His hearers to "enter by the narrow gate" or to enter on a life of commitment to God or the way of salvation. What He then says in allegorical language compares the popularity of life in the kingdom with that of the life of nonbelievers. The "gates" are named before the "ways" and evidently lead into the ways rather than coming at the end of them, as is popularly taught. The Greek word for *gate* refers to a city or a palace gate that leads into a passageway. Reference seems to be to a mansion with a large main entrance gate and a narrow entrance known to a few. One may easily drift through the large portal with the crowd and may carry through it his self-righteousness and vices; but this gate and passage "leads to destruction," utter, final ruin—not annihilation, for the term never means that.

Narrow is the gate by which entrance to eternal life is obtained. "Anything goes" is not the spirit here. One comes in the restricted manner that God Himself dictates, through faith in the sacrifice of Christ. No other approach is acceptable. Jesus Himself is both the Gate (John 10:9) and the Way (John 14:6). There is only one way as far as God is concerned; early Christians were called those of "the way" (Acts 9:2; 19:9,23; 22:4; 24:14,22).

Verses 15-20 warn against false guides who propose to direct us and of course would lead us through the wide gate. These false teachers with their own formulas of truth make the narrow way doubly hard to find because at first sight their teaching seems to bear resemblance to the truth. These false prophets only "come to you"; they are not sent. They pretend to be gentle sheep but actually are rapacious wolves, seeking to devour or destroy you. They must have a gentle, plausible appearance in order to persuade people to receive their message, but the falseness of their teaching will become evident eventually. "By their fruit you will recognize them" (NIV) refers according to some commentators to doctrines of false prophets and according to others to their works. Some observe that it is hard to distinguish genuine from hypocritical works and therefore one must carefully test the teachings of the false prophets by the Word of God. Others argue that their doctrines eventually produce a perverted morality and thus betray the error of their ways. Perhaps it would not be wrong to suggest a combination of the two.

The question of verse 16 serves as an introduction to the simile of verses 17-20, which teaches the relationship of the tree to the nature of its fruit. "Every tree not producing good fruit" is to be removed from the orchard so it does not infect the others. "Throw it into the fire" evidently refers to the judgment awaiting false teachers. Apparently the warning issued in this passage is not necessarily directed against the Pharisees but against all false prophets that will try to mislead the disciples in the future. Verses 21-23 seem to support such a conclusion.

The problem of identifying false teachers is compounded by the fact that some of them perform spectacular deeds in Christ's name, and a few of them may even be self-deceived into thinking that doing good works in Jesus' name guarantees them a seat in heaven (vv. 21-23). They will claim to have prophesied or taught publicly in His name, to have used His name in the formula of exorcism, and to have performed miracles in His power. But this is all just lip service, without a true recognition of His lordship, without a true commitment in their hearts to His moral and spiritual demands. So He will unmask them: "I never knew you"— they were not even acquaintances, let alone friends (cf. Luke 13:26). "Depart from me" speaks of the finality of judgment (cf. 25:41). To give authority to His statement, Jesus calls God "my Father," claims divine sonship, and sets Himself up as the final judge of all mankind.

4. *The two builders* (7:24-27). Jesus' sermon concludes with a parable of the two builders, which underlines the necessity of building on the right foundation in the spiritual as in the material realm. The picture is not of two men deliberately selecting foundations but of one carefully choosing and preparing his foundation (cf. Luke 6:48) and the other neglecting the importance of having any at all. The one who builds "on the rock" Jesus Christ (1 Cor. 3:11), accepts His words and puts them into practice. "These words of mine" must refer to the sermon just delivered (Matt. 5–7).

The person who builds on the foundation of faith in Christ a superstructure of Christian character and good works can withstand the storms "of misunderstanding and disappointment, of cynicism and doubt, of suffering and persecution, when they threaten to overwhelm him" (Tasker, p. 84).

Conversely, the one who has no real faith in Christ may build a life which in many ways is similar to that of a believer and may appear to be as solid. But the superstructure is built on sand—an empty profession and externalism—and there is no foundation to give support to the house in time of adversity, hence the total collapse, like a house of cards. In a sense, what is said here compares to the judgment scene above. Just as some may counterfeit a religious experience, others may build superstructures or lives much like those of believers. The destruction of the house in the latter case is similar to the judgment rendered in the former. Thus Jesus' sermon ended on a somber note.

5. *Concluding observations* (7:28-29). "When Jesus had finished these words, the multitudes were dumbfounded." This verse indicates that Matthew 5–7 should be regarded as a unit and that the passage is not a collection of sayings excerpted from a whole period of Jesus' ministry. Lenski calls attention to the psychological effect of the moment. As long as Jesus spoke, He commanded rapt attention. But when He finished, His hearers relaxed and amazement swept over them as they reflected on what He had been saying (p. 314). "He was teaching," He kept on teaching as one with authority ("I say unto you") instead of "as their scribes," who quoted learned rabbis and haggled over minute points of the law. Moreover, Jesus scorned hypocrisy and insisted on right relationship to God and works of true piety flowing from that relationship. This was a revolutionary approach; they had gotten used to hypocrisy in the conduct of their religious leaders.

For Futher Study

1. Using a concordance, make a study of Scripture passages using "meek" or "meekness" to discover the connotations of this concept in the Bible.

2. Using dictionaries, encyclopedias, or other helps, study the concept of hunger to gain a fuller appreciation of what may be involved in hungering after righteousness.

3. With the help of encyclopedias or even physics books, study the properties of light to see what it means for Christ or a Christian to be the light of the world.

4. With the help of a concordance, study the practice of fasting in Scripture. Under what circumstances was it done? Is fasting for today? If so, under what conditions should it be done?

5. What principles for prayer can you add to those indicated in Matthew 6:5-15; 7:7-12.

Chapter 5

Demonstration of the Messiah's Power
(Matthew 8:1–9:34)

In his topical rather than chronological arrangement, Matthew next introduces some of the credentials of the Messiah by presenting a series of miracles. His grouping of ten specific miracles and allusion to many others demonstrates Jesus' power over sickness, nature, demons, and death. Analysis of the literary structure of chapters 8 and 9 reveals three series of miraculous works (8:1-17; 8:23–9:8; 9:18-33a), each followed by response or reaction (8:18-22; 9:9-17; 9:33b-34). This arrangement would lend itself to the instruction of Jewish converts who gathered in study groups.

A. First Series of Miracles (8:1-17)

1. *Cleansing the leper* (8:1-4). Evidently this first miracle belongs here chronologically: "When he came down from the mountainside" (v. 1). Mark (1:40-45) and Luke (5:12-16), who also report this miracle, are inexact about the time of its occurrence. "A man with leprosy came." This loathsome disease is hard to equate with modern diseases; suffice it to say that it was incurable and cut off those who contracted it from all normal social involvements. The leper "prostrated himself" to the ground as an inferior seeking a favor from a superior. "Lord" should not be viewed as implying more than master, rabbi, or sir.

The faith of the leper was examplary, for he did not say, "If you can," but "If you will," make me clean. The action of the Savior was remarkable, for He touched the untouchable and healed him instantly. The command of the Savior was significant, for He told the leper to report to the priest for ceremonial cleansing, thus demonstrating His respect for the Mosaic law.

69

"Tell no one" was designed not to avoid publicity because a crowd had witnessed the healing. Rather, Jesus wanted the man to hold back on talking about his good fortune until he had been to the priest to be declared clean. The reason for this course of action presumably was for the benefit of the priest, the crowd, and the man. "Then" could refer either to the priest or the crowd. Thus the man was to rush to the priest to tell his own story of his healing before the priest heard a garbled version of what had happened and would be prejudiced against him. The story of healing certainly would be a witness to unbelieving priests. And it would be a witness to the crowd if the priest declared the man clean and approved an official version of what had happened. Moreover, it was important to the healed man because an official declaration of healing would take away the man's social stigma and restore to him the ability to move freely in society again. For "the gift that Moses commanded," see Leviticus 14:4,10,21-22.

2. *Healing the centurion's servant* (8:5-13). Comparison with the parallel account in Luke 7:1-10 leads to the conclusion that this centurion did not come before Jesus in person but through intermediaries. Though a Roman military man, he had befriended the Jews and had been instrumental in construction of the Capernaum synagogue. Elders of that synagogue now came to bring his request for healing of his servant who was "paralyzed and in terrible suffering" (NIV). In response to the request, Jesus started out for the centurion's house. But the centurion sent word that he did not consider himself worthy to receive a visit from Jesus. With a burst of faith, he declared his confidence in the ability of the Master to heal by remote control: "Just say the word." The meaning of verse 9 is that just as the centurion (a commander of one hundred men) issued orders and expected them to be obeyed, so he believed that Jesus who was infinitely more powerful would have His orders obeyed.

Jesus was filled with admiration for the centurion's faith, which was greater than any He had encountered among the Jews. This gave Him occasion to observe that though the kingdom was offered primarily to the Jews, hosts of Gentiles will participate in it. They will do so during the thousands of years that the kingdom is in its spiritual form and to an even greater degree when the messianic kingdom is established on earth and every knee shall bow to Christ and every tongue shall confess Him as Lord. The casting out of "sons of the kingdom" does not mean that believers are to be sent to perdition but only indicates that a natural-born Jew who fails to exercise faith in Christ will discover that "mere race is not sufficient qualification for Christ's kingdom" (Kent, p. 942).

Then Jesus pronounced the word of healing and the centurion's servant was healed "at that very hour." The inclusion of this miracle here serves not only to accredit the message and ministry of the Messiah but also to demonstrate God's concern for all sinful human beings—Jew and Gentile—and to declare the basis on which they will all enter the kingdom: by faith.

3. *Healing Peter's mother-in-law* (8:14-17). As is clear from parallel accounts in Mark 1:29-34 and Luke 4:38-41, this miracle took place on the Sabbath after the morning synagogue service. Jesus went to the house of Simon and Andrew with at least James and John. There Peter's mother-in-law lay sick of a fever, and some in the household brought her need to the Master's attention—certainly with a view to His doing something about it. Jesus took her by the hand to raise her up; and as soon as He touched her, the fever left and she got up and waited on them.

Several observations may be made about this healing:

1. Jesus was not averse to doing the work of healing on the Sabbath when human need called for it.

2. If Jesus healed Simon's mother-in-law, Simon was married—contrary to Roman Catholic teaching.

3. This illness presumably was not as incurable as in the case of the two previously reported miracles. But it was a miracle nonetheless because Jesus healed her of her high fever immediately, and she required no period of rest and recovery before she began to wait on the assembled guests.

4. Evidently word quickly spread all over the fishing village of Capernaum, even though it was the Sabbath. Houses were so tightly compacted that this was possible without the inhabitants' having to walk around to tell the news. Townsfolk respected the Sabbath, however, and waited until sundown to bring their sick and demon-possessed to Jesus. He healed all who came but none were singled out for special mention. A total of thirty-five miracles are described in some detail in the Gospels; in addition, several mass or general healings are recorded. Those in Matthew alone include 4:23-24; 8:16; 9:35; 11:20-24; 12:15; 14:14,36; 15:30; 19:2; 21:14. Presumably others occurred that the writer did not report. The healing of many in this passage is seen as partial fulfillment of Isaiah 53:4. Such healing could occur as Jesus bore the sin of man on the cross and so dealt with disease, one of sin's effects.

B. First Response (8:18-22)

These verses show two responses to the wonder-working ministry of Jesus. It is unnecessary to struggle with their chronological placement or exact relation to the parallel account in Luke 9:57-62 in order to discover their message for us. It is not clear whether the first man, one of the scribes, was already in some sense a follower of Jesus; presumably he was only a prospective disciple. Jesus evidently was warning against overconfident, ill-considered decisions to follow Him. He pointed out that discipleship costs something, not the least of which is physical privation. Jesus did not even have a temporary place of residence as foxes and birds do. "Son of man" was Jesus' usual designation of Himself; probably the term was derived from Daniel 7:13-14. It must be considered equal to "Son of God."

The second man Jesus conversed with is described as already being a "disciple," but he wanted to put off full commitment to Christ and the business of the kingdom. One should not view burial of one's father in the Western sense. In the first place, Jews buried their dead on the day of their demise. Probably the issue of delay in serving Jesus would not have come up if the man's father were already dead, for the funeral would have occurred within hours at most. Second, in New Testament times a remark like this would have involved living with an aged or infirm father for an extended period of time until his demise and burial. The urgency of the business of the kingdom, of working in fields already "white unto harvest," would not permit this kind of delay. "Let the dead bury their own dead" (NIV) is another way of saying, "Let those who are spiritually dead care for those who are spiritually dead; you who are spiritually alive need to be about the business of the kingdom." It is not clear whether either or both of these men accepted the word of the Master and gave themselves to full discipleship or whether they "went away sorrowful" (Matt. 19:22).

C. Second Series of Miracles (8:23–9:8)

1. *Calming the storm* (8:23-27). Mark 4:36-41 and Luke 8:22-25 make it clear that this narrative took place at the end of a day of teaching and ministering to the crowds and fits chronologically after the parables of Matthew 13. Seeking some release from the hectic pace, Jesus and His disciples got into "the ship" and sailed from the area of Capernaum to the eastern shore of the Sea of Galilee. Since the sea is less than eight

miles in width, the journey was not a long one. "The ship" (not "a ship") was used frequently by Jesus and the disciples and presumably belonged to the partnership of Peter, Andrew, James, and John.

Exhausted, Jesus fell asleep. Soon one of those terrible storms arose that periodically hits the Sea of Galilee almost without warning. Winds funnel through the passes between adjacent hills and descend onto the surface of the lake (about 700 feet below sea level) churning the waters furiously. This must have been a particularly bad storm because Matthew uses the term *seismos* (elsewhere "earthquake") to describe "the tempest." In spite of the fact that great waves broke over the boat, began to fill it, and threatened to sink it, Jesus "continued to sleep."

The fear of these seasoned fishermen also indicates the severity of the storm. Having exhausted their own resources, in desperation they woke Jesus, crying, "Lord, save us; we are going down!" (Williams). These men of the sea committed themselves into the hands of the Carpenter of Nazareth who had never sailed a boat! Then, if one follows the order of Mark and Luke, Jesus stilled the winds and waves with a word, and immediately all was calm. Storms sometimes do suddenly cease but waters remain choppy for a while; a miracle was evident on this occasion because the waters too became calm. What contrasts: the terrified disciples and the composed Master, the raging tempest and the total calm!

Then Jesus rebuked the disciples, "How frightened you are, men of little faith!" (Lenski, p. 347). Their fear revealed lack of faith. Perhaps rebuke rested on the fact that "if He was in the boat with them, all must be well" (Tasker, p. 93) or that He expected more of them because they had already experienced His miraculous power in so many other ways. Moreover, He had commanded this trip to the other side, and they should have trusted Him to get them across. Here is further evidence that being in God's will does not make one immune from serious difficulty. Their response? They were "amazed" or "dumbfounded." "What kind of man is this, that even the winds and sea obey him?" No response is recorded in any of the three Gospels. All sorts of explanations may be given for healing from physical ailments, but only God has complete control over nature.

2. *Casting out demons* (8:28-34). So far miracles selected have demonstrated Jesus' power over disease, physical deformity, and the natural world. Next Matthew shows Jesus' control over the world of evil spirits. In this account Jesus heals two demon-possessed men, but in

Mark 5:1-20 and Luke 8:26-39 only the more vocal of the two figures is mentioned in the narrative. The location of this event was on the southeastern shore of the Sea of Galilee. There two naked demon-possessed men lived in caves which served as tombs. Their ferocity made the area virtually impassable to travelers.

Demons and their control over human beings are presented as being very real in the New Testament, and demon possession is not to be dismissed either on mission fields in some of the underdeveloped countries or the industrial West today. One should not go to the extreme either of explaining all demon-possession as mental illness or concluding that all mental illness is demon-possession.

Commonly striking fear into others, the demons became victims of fear themselves. "What do you want with us, Son of God? they shouted" (NIV). Devils believe and tremble (James 2:19); they recognize the Son of God though human beings may not. They know that their doom is sure and have some idea of when it will occur. And they obey Jesus. But in this case, as comes clear from accounts in the other Gospels, after Jesus commanded them to come out of the men, they delayed slightly and asked a favor. They did not want to be sent back into the abyss (Luke 8:31) and so sought another embodiment; entrance into another human being would have been out of the question under the circumstances.

Their request to be sent away into the swine cannot really be explained. It has been suggested that as morally and spiritually unclean, the demons had affinity with the unclean swine. Also, it is possible that under Satan's direction they anticipated an opportunity to hinder Jesus' ministry in this region. Jesus granted the demons' request; they entered into the swine, drove them down a slope into the water, and destroyed them. It is staggering to contemplate how many demons may have possessed the two unfortunate Gadarenes.

The request of the demons and their subsequent action absolved Jesus from any direct responsibility for destruction of property; He did not initiate the idea or command the action. Moreover, probably the owners were Jews who were illegally raising hogs. This conclusion is reached from the fact that Jesus ministered almost exclusively to Jews, the event took place in the territory of Herod Philip, and the owners brought no complaint or request for redress.

Frightened by the violence of the moment and the destruction of valuable property for which they were resonsible, the swineherds fled to the nearby town to make a report to their employers. They also went into great detail ("told everything") with the townsfolk about all the dramatic events that had just occurred. Curious and disturbed, virtually the entire population came to see Jesus, the restored demoniacs, and the dead pigs floating in the water. Evidently because they feared further losses to themselves, they asked Jesus to leave their area, which He did. But He left behind the two restored men to herald abroad a message concerning Jesus and His kingdom, which they did faithfully (Mark 5:20). This was not contrary to Jesus' usual desire to avoid unnecessary publicity that would bring out the kind of crowds which only impeded His ministry. In this case He would not be around to gather crowds.

3. *Healing a paralytic* (9:1-8). Leaving the eastern shore of the Sea of Galilee at the request of the Gadarenes, Jesus took ship (evidently the same one He came on) and sailed to Capernaum, "his own city." Capernaum is so-called only here and is distinguished as a place where He was welcome as opposed to the town from which He had just been expelled.

In fact, Jesus was so thronged in Capernaum that the only way four men could get their paralytic friend to Him was to tear up the roof over Jesus' head and lower him into Jesus' presence on his portable bed. Matthew omits much of the drama and detail of the event (see Mark 2:3-12; Luke 5:18-26) and concentrates on the vital issues. "Their faith" refers not only to the faith of the four—a faith which overcomes all obstacles—but also to that of the paralytic. The faith of the latter also must be meant because one cannot have saving faith for another, and Jesus declares the sins of the paralytic forgiven. It is clear from this narrative that the paralytic's physical condition had something to do with his spiritual condition. Some would claim that his disability was a result of sin. Others consider such an assumption risky and conclude that his condition had brought on a serious reflection on his spiritual condition or a preoccupation with it.

Scribes (and other Pharisees) from Jerusalem, Judea, and Galilee had been stalking Jesus to accumulate evidence against Him. At this point they believed they had it. "Within themselves" they were saying Jesus was guilty of blasphemy because by their standards Jesus was a mere man and He was taking upon Himself the prerogative of forgiving sin; only God can do that. Not only did He claim the divine right to forgive sins, but He exercised the divine power to read the thoughts of His observers. Unmasking their evil intent, He said in effect, "Which requires less effort, to forgive sins or to heal? Both require the power of God." Of course the forgiveness of sins is not verifiable by sensory proof as an overt act of healing is. Jesus connected the two and used the one as evidence of the other.

When the crowds witnessed this miracle, "they were frightened" or "filled with awe," overcome with the kind of reverential fear that a sinner experiences in the presence of almighty God. But they praised God because of the great benefits His mighty presence bestowed. Evidently they had witnessed His performance of many miracles and recognized God's power exercised in and through the works of Jesus. This miracle demonstrates Jesus' power to heal disease and forgive sin as the two previous ones showed His control over nature and the world of demons.

D. Second Response (9:9-17)

1. *Matthew* (9:9-10). In Matthew 9:9-17 there is a threefold response to Jesus and His wonderful works: that of Matthew, the Pharisees, and John's disciples. As Jesus left His house after healing the paralytic, He passed Matthew's tax office at Capernaum. Matthew was in the employ of the Roman occupation government as a collector of customs duties on goods that came from the East, either by caravan route or across the Sea of Galilee. Therefore he would have been despised by the Jews of his community. Mark 2:14 and Luke 5:27 call him Levi, perhaps his original name; Matthew is thought to be the name adopted after his conversion.

A public figure like Matthew hardly could have been unaware of Jesus and His ministry, but what specific preparation he may have had for his call to discipleship is not known. He made a clean break with his past and left his former employment. Thereafter he threw a banquet at his house (Luke 5:29) to which he invited tax gatherers and sinners and Jesus, presumably so the Master would have a chance to win them to Himself. "Sinners" refers to those who did not live by the Mosaic law and were either regarded as impure by the Pharisees or actually lived disreputable lives.

2. *The Pharisees* (9:11-13). After the dinner at Matthew's house the Pharisees criticized Jesus for associating with publicans and sinners— outcasts. This they did in conversation with the disciples, not in direct confrontation. When Jesus learned of their questioning, He addressed the Pharisees directly. Accepting their own estimate of themselves as

righteous before the law or spiritually well and of publicans and sinners as unrighteous or spiritually sick, He declared that His ministry as the Great Physician must be to the sick. But then Jesus made it clear that He did not really consider the Pharisees to be righteous.

"Go and learn what this means" shows that evidently they did not know. Next He quoted Hosea 6:6, which they should have known: "I desire compassion and not [mere] sacrifice." Jesus wanted to show pity or compassion: "I have come to call sinners." He did not come to hobnob with publicans and sinners as one of their kind but to call them to a higher spiritual plane. All the Pharisees did was engage in fastidious law keeping ("sacrifice") and cold-hearted ostracism of those who needed mercy and spiritual help.

3. *John's disciples* (9:14-17). Next some disciples of John the Baptist came to question Jesus. John did not send them because he was in prison on the other side of the Jordan River. Disciples of John like the Pharisees had added to the required fast on the Day of Atonement (e.g., Lev. 23:27), fasting on Mondays and Thursdays. Hence they were affronted by the feast at Matthew's house, evidently on one of their fast days. Jesus' answer was couched in John's own figure of speech (John 3:29). Friends of the bridegroom do not fast at a wedding in the presence of the bridegroom, but they will fast (mourn) when the bridegroom (Jesus) is snatched away from them by violent death.

Then Jesus changed the figure of speech. No one patches an old garment, which is thoroughly shrunk by many washings, with a new unshrunk piece of cloth. If he does, when that garment is washed the new cloth will shrink and create a worse tear. Likewise, one does not put unfermented grape juice into old wineskins. Old wineskins (made from goat hides) have been stretched just about to the limit by a previous fermentation process. If they are used for another fermentation process, they will be stretched beyond the breaking point and will spill their contents on the ground.

What Jesus was saying is that He was not merely patching up contemporary Judaism or Pharisaism but was superseding it with a new way of grace and faith. As is clear from many passages, however, He was not suggesting that the principles and doctrines of Old Testament times should be done away. The dead, restrictive ritualism that had evolved in Judaism is what had to go, in favor of a new, freer life in the Spirit.

E. Third Series of Miracles (9:18-33a)

1. *Raising a dead girl and healing a sick woman* (9:18-26). As is true with other miracles reported in Matthew 8–9, the account of these two is greatly telescoped (compare Mark 5:22-43; Luke 8:41-56). Matthew went quickly to the heart of the matter and demonstrated the wonder-working power of the Messiah. While Jesus was still talking with the disciples of John, Jairus, a ruler of the synagogue, evidently of Capernaum, prostrated himself at Jesus' feet in oriental fashion and presented his request for the healing of his daughter.

"Has just died" is not really at variance with Mark and Luke, who report him as saying his daughter was at the point of death. Matthew omits the second stage of the account, when word of the girl's death is brought to the father. What we have here is the situation as it confronts the Messiah: a dead person needs to be brought back to life. The father's faith is considerable; he believes that though the case is hopeless from a human standpoint, the girl will live if Jesus merely lays His hand of healing upon her as He had upon others.

Jesus and His disciples promptly followed Jairus. On the way a woman who had been "suffering with a hemorrhage for twelve years" wormed her way through the crowd with the hope of touching the fringe or tassel of His robe. This shows Jesus' compliance with Old Testament instructions about dress (Num. 15:38; Deut. 22:12), an important detail in a book designed especially for Jewish readers. The woman touched Him and was healed, but she did not slip away unnoticed. Jesus wanted her to know that her "faith has restored" her rather than any magical powers of His clothing. And He wanted the crowd to witness another evidence of His power. He is the master of the impossible. Here He heals a woman with an incurable disease immediately ("from that moment"); next He will raise a girl who has already died!

When Jesus arrived at Jairus' house, a typical Jewish mourning was in progress. Only Matthew mentions the "flute-players," an indication that he was writing for those familiar with Jewish mourning customs. These musicians accompanied hired wailing women who created a terrible din. Jesus said, "Go away. The girl is not dead but asleep" (NIV). Of course those gathered ridiculed Him. Jesus evidently meant to indicate here, as in the case of Lazarus, who had been dead four days (John 11:11,14,17), the temporary nature of death and His intention of awaking the dead one. Again Matthew abbreviates following events, focusing instead on the magnificent ability of the Messiah even to raise the dead! Perhaps the family did obey the command not to publicize exactly what had happened (Mark 5:43; Luke 8:56); but of course many others knew the net result, for the girl walked among them. Hence the whole region heard about it.

2. *Healing the blind* (9:27-31). After Jesus left Jairus' house and proceeded toward His own place of residence, two blind men began to follow Him and to yell repeatedly, "Have mercy on us, son of David." "Son of David" is a messianic designation with political significance, and presumably for that reason Jesus paid no attention to the men. Any effort to cast Him in the role of a Messiah this early in His ministry might short-circuit His ministry.

When Jesus came into "the house" (His residence in Capernaum, possibly Peter's house), however, He was willing to give them attention privately. In asking, "Do you believe that I can do this?" Jesus no doubt sought to deepen their faith and perhaps also to center it more fully on His divine person and power rather than His messianic office. Through His gracious touch He gave the blind assurance of His intent to meet their need. "According to your faith" probably should be understood to signify "in response to your faith," for healing does not come in exact proportion to faith. In fact, sometimes Jesus healed to engender faith. "Be it done to you": instantaneously is the force of the Greek. Opened eyes signifies restoration to perfect sight as closed eyes indicates blindness.

"Jesus sternly ordered them," severely warned them, "See that nobody knows it" (Williams). Probably the "it" does not refer to telling people that Jesus had performed a miracle, for the healed men henceforth would live normal lives and their friends and acquaintances would demand information about their healing. Rather, "the object must be that Jesus is not to be proclaimed as the Son of David" (Lenski, p. 379). Of course they could not keep silent about their marvelous good fortune.

3. *Healing the dumb demoniac* (9:32-33a). As the two healed blind men went out, others brought a man whose power of speech had been impeded by demon possession. Comparison of this case of demon possession with others mentioned in Scripture (e.g., Matt. 8:28) indicates that demonic control affects human beings in different ways. Released from the grip of demons, the man "spoke." The account is unembellished but it is striking in its simplicity.

F. Third Response (9:33b-34)

"The crowds were amazed" must refer to the general response to Jesus' miraculous works among the populace of Galilee, for there were no crowds present at the deliverance of the man struck dumb; and it was not highlighted as a major miracle. In contrast, the conniving, scurrilously critical Pharisees ignored the larger view and focused on the one miracle: "It is by the help of the prince of the demons that He drives them out" (Williams). Evidently they could not even venture a suggestion to explain away His other miracles. It is not clear whether the Pharisees made this charge of His being in league with demons before a crowd or only among themselves. Presumably they did not utter it or even think it in Jesus' presence because He did not respond to it as He did later in Matthew 12:24-30.

For Further Study

1. Read articles on leprosy in at least two Bible encyclopedias.

2. Make a comparison study of the miracles in Matthew 8 and 9, noting the categories over which Jesus exercised power (nature, disease, etc.), Jesus' method, response of the restored, response of the onlookers.

3. What did you learn about the disciples in these two chapters?

4. What opposition did Jesus encounter?

5. What concepts or doctrines did Jesus enunciate in these chapters?

Chapter 6

The Messiah and His Kingdom Preachers
(Matthew 9:35–11:1)

In the logical development of an account of Jesus' ministry, Matthew now turns from a demonstration of the effect of that ministry on the multitudes to the need for expanding His efforts. Of course Jesus could not do the job alone. Therefore He elevated the disciples from the level of observers to that of co-workers or apprentices. As He sent them out to spread the gospel of the kingdom, He instructed them how to conduct themselves, warned them of opposition, and exhorted them to total dedication to Himself and His cause.

A. Their Call (9:35–10:4)

1. *Need for workers* (9:35-38). As Jesus went on a long preaching and healing tour throughout Galilee, His "heart was stirred" by the spiritual condition of the people, who were as "sheep without a shepherd," with no one to lead and care for them. Among the multitudes neglected by the national teachers, and therefore without a shepherd, were a great many who had been impressed by the ministry of Jesus or had seeking hearts or had become receptive because of the extremity of their need. These could be brought into the kingdom if someone would present the gospel to them. Jesus viewed such as ripe fields of grain ready for harvest: "The harvest is plentiful" but unfortunately "the workers are few."

With this thought Matthew makes the transition to the next section, the commissioning of the apostles. They are to pray the "Lord of the harvest," God who is the great Lord and proprietor of all and controls its management ("my Father is the husbandman," John 15:1), that He will "thrust forth" workers. And they will help to answer their own prayers.

2. *Commission of the Twelve* (10:1-4). Jesus called the Twelve before Him to receive their commission. "Power" translates a Greek word which means both power and authority (cf. Luke 9:1 where two words appear for greater explicitness); He qualified and authorized them "over" or "against unclean spirits." "All diseases" and "all sickness" is comprehensive. It is important to note that Jesus distinguished between disease and demon possession. The Twelve were called "apostles," not just learners (disciples) but sent ones or commissioned ones.

The following list is grouped in pairs, implying that they went out two by two. Simon's name always appears first in lists of the apostles, Judas Iscariot's always last. The first four are two pairs of brothers. Bartholomew means son of Tolmai (Ptolemy) and is evidently a family surname. He is to be equated with Nathanael of Cana; his name follows Philip in Mark's and Luke's list of the Twelve (cf. Mark 3:16-19; Luke 6:14-16). Matthew the publican or tax-gatherer is so-called only in this Gospel, probably to demonstrate the great grace he had received in his salvation. Thaddeus apparently had two other names: Lebbeus and Judas (John 14:22). Simon the Canaanite (Cananaean) is properly rendered "zealot"; before his conversion he must have been a member of the militantly nationalistic sect of zealots. "Iscariot" means man of Kerioth, a town in Judah.

B. Their Calling (10:5–11:1)

1. *Personal instructions* (10:5-15). Instructions given here evidently apply to this mission only and are not to be regarded as permanent. Certainly the prohibition against preaching to Samaritans (racial half-breeds) could not be valid after the giving of the Great Commission (Matt. 28:19-20) or Jesus' great ascension promise (Acts 1:8). Details concerning what the apostles should or should not take seems to have little relevance for the post-Pentecostal period. They were to go out briefly then and were to make little provision for the mission. That the disciples did not carry on this way normally is evident from the fact that Judas was the treasurer of the group and managed the common treasury, which received donations from some of the women whom Jesus healed (Luke 8:2-3), as well as others.

The mission to "the lost sheep of the house of Israel" was to present to them the messianic kingdom of heaven. To the earlier comprehensive statement on healing, verse 8 adds a word about raising the dead, though there is no evidence that the disciples did so on this tour. These marvelous works served to accredit the messengers and their message, as they did for Jesus Himself. "Freely give" means do not accept pay of any kind for the exercise of these powers or for any other service rendered.

Next Jesus said, in effect, that they were not to make any special preparations for this journey. They were not to take any money or extra clothing or a traveling bag. From a comparison with Mark 6:8-9, it is evident that verse 10 means they could use the sandals or walking stick they already had but were not to get new ones. This was to be an exercise of faith. "The worker is worthy of his maintenance"; grateful recipients of their ministry would provide for them.

Jesus next instructed the Twelve as to how they were to proceed (vv. 11-15). As they entered any town or village to conduct their ministry, they were to look for some congenial family who was receptive to the truth and would invite them to stay in their home. Once they established such residence, they were not to move about in an effort to better their situation. When they went to such a house, they were to "salute it," show it the usual civilities. If compatibility continued because of a general receptivity to the truth, they were to remain. If their host became antagonistic to the gospel on learning more of what it entailed, they were to leave and accept other accommodations.

If after some ministry in a home or a town, antagonism forced them to leave, "on leaving shake off the dust of your feet" as a symbolic demonstration that the truth was not welcome there. This "would vividly and yet solemnly portray the disciples' freedom from involvement in their opponents' guilt and coming judgment" (Kent, p. 946). As bad as Sodom and Gomorrah were, they would be treated as less criminal in the judgment "than those places which, though morally respectable, reject the Gospel message and affront those that bear it" (Brown, p. 62).

2. *Coming persecutions* (10:16-31). These verses and those that follow concern the current mission only in part; evidently they look out into the apostolic history as recorded in the Book of Acts and even beyond down to the end of the age. "I myself send you forth as sheep among wolves," Jesus said. "I" is in the emphatic position; "send you forth" (*apostellō*, the word from which "apostle" is derived), means commission or send on a mission. Since the disciples were identified

with Him, they could expect not only His power but the onus that comes with bearing His name.

While on this mission, the disciples would find themselves as "sheep" (defenseless ones) among "wolves" (viciously wicked opponents). In facing such, their conduct was to be characterized by the "prudence of serpents" (wary, sharp-sighted, quick to discern danger) and the "guilelessness of doves" (innocent, so they have no just cause against them).

"Be on guard," to avoid giving unnecessary offense and thus stirring needless anger against you, Jesus warned. "Councils" evidently refers to local Jewish courts, synagogue tribunals, which had the power to order flogging (e.g., Acts 22:19; 26:11). Verse 18 looks beyond the immediate mission into the apostolic age when these and other servants of God would face political (Gentile) persecution. "Governors," provincial rulers (such as Felix and Festus at Caesarea, Acts 24–25; Gallio at Corinth, Acts 18:12-17; or the authorities at Thessalonica, Acts 17:6) and "kings" (as Herod Agrippa or Caesar) would have power to administer more serious punishments—even the death penalty.

"On my account" shows the suffering is for Christ. As a result of this persecution, a testimony will be given to "them" (the Jews who instigate the attacks) and "Gentiles" because every time a believer is brought before a tribunal for examination and/or trial, the charge on which he is brought (believing or preaching the gospel) is rehearsed and investigated.

When you are put on trial for your faith, "do not worry about what to say or how to say it," either the content or the manner of the defense. It is of course impossible to devise hypothetical defenses ahead of time because one cannot anticipate the exact time of apprehension, the nature of accusation, or the course of a trial. "It shall be given you": the promise of aid is unequivocal. Bearing His name may bring suffering but witness is accompanied by divine energizing. The Holy Spirit Himself provides utterance, but He does not merely dictate words, for He will speak "in you" (not "through you")—not violating but employing the human mind and personality.

Frightful cases of betrayal are predicted, when even members of one's family may present information against him to the authorities (v. 21). But even though all may hate the believer, he is not to "draw back unto perdition" (Heb. 10:39); he is to endure "to the end" as an evidence of the reality of his faith. Enduring to the end might be interpreted as applying to the end of life, but the promise seems better related to the tribulation context as it appears in Matthew 24:13 (see discussion). "When persecuted, flee." The individual is not to seek martyrdom; flight to preserve life is not incompatible either with courage or loyalty to the gospel.

The last half of verse 23 is very difficult to interpret. Perhaps it means that the Son of man (Christ) would come at the end time, before all the towns of Israel are thoroughly evangelized. If verse 22 applies to a tribulation context, perhaps this one does too (see discussion of Matt. 24:8-31).

The axiomatic statement of verse 24 is meant to indicate the relationship between Jesus and His disciples. The joining of disciples to Jesus in the intimate relationship of disciples to their teachers or slaves to their lords means that they will be "as" He, sharing in what is characteristic of His experience. If the enemies (Pharisees and others) of the "lord of the house" engage in vicious slander, calling Him "Beelzebub," a term for Satan (Matt. 12:24), they will heap worse abuse on the "members of his household" because they are weaker and more vulnerable.

"Do do not be afraid of them." You are, after all, members of the household, who can count on the Lord of the house. Furthermore, in the judgment He will cast the searchlight of His justice on all things hidden and will give everyone his due (1 Cor. 4:5). Fear can only paralyze and prevent one from engaging in an effective ministry. Jesus said, "What I teach you now in private, broadcast in the future from the housetops"—easy to do in Palestine, where the houses were low and flat-roofed. To the one who may fear losing his life in such a ministry, Jesus replied that persecutors may kill the body but "after that can do no more" (Luke 12:4 NIV); they "cannot kill the soul." "But keep on fearing Him who can destroy the soul and body in hell." One is to continue to reverence or worship God, who can reach beyond the grave to exercise judgment. "Him" cannot refer to Satan who himself will be punished there. "Soul and body in hell" clearly teaches that future punishment will involve both the material and immaterial part of the unsaved. Evidently at the Great White Throne judgment (Rev. 20:11-15) the unregenerate dead will be resurrected and given immortal bodies which will then suffer in eternal torment.

In verses 29-31 Jesus encourages the disciples not to be afraid because God's watch-care and concern, which extends to the minutest details of His creation, certainly will overshadow them. Though two "sparrows" are so cheap when sold for meat that they go for an *assarion*, a very insignificant copper coin, they do not fall to the ground without God's permission. "Your Father" hints at the disciples' greater claim on the provision of God. Even every one of the hairs of one's head, without exception, has been counted and one is not lost unobserved. So if God is involved to that extent with His creation, His children need not fear any lack of attention to their protection.

3. *Demand for total dedication* (10:32-39). As a deterrent to yielding to persecution, and in line with His demand for the total dedication of His followers, Jesus made reference to the final judgment. "Confesses me" is literally "confesses in me." The construction teaches that confession arises out of union with Christ. Vincent summarizes the thought as "abide in me, and being in me, confess me" (Vol. I, p. 61). This construction is balanced by the declaration, "I will confess in him"; Christ abides in the true believer (cf. John 17:23). The one who publicly recognizes Jesus as Lord and Savior here below will enjoy Christ's recognition of him before the Father—now as He intercedes for us (Heb. 7:25) and in the future judgment. Conversely, those destitute of grace and not in Christ and who deny Him will be disowned at the judgment.

Verse 34 seems at first glance to contradict many other passages of Scripture. For example, Christ came as the Prince of Peace; the angels sang "peace on earth" at His birth; and His disciples were to preach peace (Matt. 10:12-13). Harmonization is possible, however, Ultimately Christ will rule over a world at peace, and even the enmity which exists in the natural world will be removed (Isa. 11:6-9). But the very coming of Christ to earth divided the world into two warring camps (brought a sword) because most people refused to accept His offer of grace. In the grip of Satan and inspired by his demonic opposition, Christ's opponents tried to destroy Him, continue to try to destroy His church, and ultimately will launch an all-out offensive against the truth and the people of God in the last days, as the Book of Revelation attests.

The opposition to truth severs intimate family ties; some accept the truth and others do not. In verse 36 Jesus gives an example of the divisiveness that will occur. Five person are living in an oriental household: a mother, father, a married son and his "bride," and an unmarried sister. The three young people are arrayed against the two older ones— in this case because of a difference in response to Christ. What Jesus says about such situations is that a disciple must not let natural affections and family ties take precedence over his stand for Christ. He must not disown Christ because of the opposition of family members and to restore peace in the family. Jesus' call for discipleship requires total devotion.

In fact, "anyone who does not take his cross and follow me is not worthy of me" (NIV). The reference is not to enduring some trial for Jesus' sake but to willingness to die for Him—willingness to serve Him so totally as to go forth even to crucifixion, bearing the cross to the place of execution, as criminals had to do. Though He was speaking to Jews and Jews did not execute by crucifixion, the disciples had seen many die in this manner at the hands of the Romans. This need not be seen as a reference to Jesus' own death. The meaning of verse 39 is that he who avoids death in the midst of persecution by denying Christ will lose his soul; but he whose devotion to Christ may result in physically dying for Him will enjoy eternal life in His presence.

4. *Reward for faithful service* (10:40-42). As Jesus concludes His address to the apostles, He assures them that those who would receive them and thus participate with them in their ministry also would have their reward. Evidently the promise is intended to apply to reception of a variety of Christian workers then and now. He who welcomes and receives you and thus the message you preach, Jesus said, is really welcoming Me and God the Father Himself. The reception which you enjoy as My ambassadors will reflect the esteem in which I am held and thus the esteem in which the Father is held. A "prophet" is not necessarily one who predicts the future but one who has been commissioned to deliver a message from heaven. "Anyone who receives a prophet because he is a prophet" (NIV), because he recognizes that his message and ministry have their source in God, shall receive such reward as a prophet has because he is actually in a sense sharing in the labors of the prophet.

Likewise, "anyone who receives a righteous man [a believer who possesses the righteousness of Christ] because he is a righteous man" (NIV) will share in whatever reward such a believer has. And in a descending scale from apostles to prophets to other Christian workers, Jesus came to include "little ones," young disciples or babes in Christ. Even the smallest service rendered to one of these because he is Christ's disciple will certainly be rewarded.

5. *Continued activity of the King* (11:1). While the apostles set

forth to do the Master's bidding, Jesus went from place to place in a ministry of His own, in "their cities," evidently towns in Galilee. Matthew says nothing about activities of the Twelve; for such detail it is necessary to turn to Mark 6:12-13 and Luke 9:6.

For Further Study

1. With the help of a Bible dictionary or Bible encyclopedia and a concordance, try to work out a brief biography for each of the twelve disciples.

2. With the help of Bible reference materials, discover how the Samaritans originated and how they differed from the Jews.

3. With the help of a Bible doctrine book and a concordance, study the subject of future rewards for believers.

4. What is involved in or implied by Jesus' title of "Prince of Peace"?

5. What good and bad effects does persecution have?

Chapter 7

Opposition to the Messiah and His Kingdom
(Matthew 11:2–12:50)

In his logical discussion of Jesus' ministry in Galilee, Matthew described the beginning of that ministry, the principles of the Messiah's kingdom, the marvelous success of His ministry, and the multiplication of His efforts and energies through the work of His disciples. As Jesus' popularity and success rose, so did opposition to Him. Opposition appeared in the imprisonment of His forerunner and the Baptist's questioning of Jesus' messianic program, the rejection of His message by various Galilean towns, the antagonism of the Pharisees—so fierce as even to accuse Him of doing wonders by the power of Satan, and the hindering efforts of His relatives.

A. Inquiry of John (11:2-19)

1. *Conversation with John's disciples* (11:2-6). While John was in prision in the fortress of Machaerus, east of the north end of the Dead Sea, he heard reports of the marvelous works of Jesus. At length he sent some of his disciples to ask whether Jesus was "the Coming One," the Messiah, or whether another was to come. Commentators often debate whether (1) John sent this message because of despondency or perplexity on his own part, (2) to confirm the faith of his own disciples, or (3) to persuade Jesus to declare His messiahship publicly. The third does not seem likely because Jesus' answer is in no way a response to an effort to force His hand. The second would preserve the consistency of John's personal faith, but verse 6 and Jesus' comment on John before the crowd seem to indicate a concern for John rather than his disciples. But even the first view does not need to implicate John in any lapse of faith as he endured the horrors of an oriental prison. He simply may have been

puzzled by the lack of fierce judgment exemplified in the conduct of the Messiah (Matt. 3:10-12).

Jesus' reply was to call attention to His miraculous works as messianic credentials (vv. 4-5). Then as a parting thrust He said, "Blessed is the man who is not entrapped [deceived] by false notions of Me." John was not to let any ideas of a vengeful, politically dominant Messiah deceive him into thinking that the Messiah would not also demonstrate His power by miracles of mercy (cf. Isa. 29:18-19; 35:5-6).

2. *Tribute to John the Baptist* (11:7-15). As the disciples of John left, Jesus began to address the bystanders who may have heard the conversation. Just in case some of them had lost their faith in John or in Christ Himself, Jesus proceeded first to pay tribute to John and soon thereafter reasserted His own power and authority. Did you go out to see a "reed swayed," a fickle waverer? The implication in that John was not a fickle, unstable person; if any thought so now they should disabuse their minds of such an illusion. Did you go out into the wilderness to see a richly dressed man, a politician's representative?—as if Jesus was about to establish an essentially political kingdom.

John's prophetic garb showed that his mission was spiritual. He was not only a prophet, in the Old Testament prophetic line, but more than a prophet; he was the forerunner of the Messiah whose ministry had been predicted some 400 years earlier (Mal. 3:1). Others had foreseen the Messiah; John had heralded the King's coming, had introduced His kingdom, and had known Him personally. Hence no other human being was greater than John; i.e., he was the greatest of the prophets, his career and work outdistanced them all.

"Yet he who is least in the kingdom of heaven is greater than he." John's imprisonment and imminent death had prevented him from being a part of the kingdom as a historical movement. Those who received what Jesus was offering them and became a part of the kingdom could be greater than John—could have greater treasures of revelation, clearer spiritual knowledge of God, and higher privileges of fellowship. John was a friend of the bridegroom (John 3:29); but the disciples, who were soon to be formed into the church at Pentecost (Acts 2), would become the bride of Christ. This pronouncement of superiority does not in any way imply that John was inferior in his faith or dedication to Christ.

"The kingdom of heaven is being taken by storm." Eager, enthusiastic persons—publicans, harlots, and the masses in general—

were flocking to Christ and seizing the kingdom for themselves as if it were a prize of war. John was the last of the Old Testament prophets to predict the coming of the messianic kingdom. If the Jews in general had been willing to accept the kingdom and the Messiah when they were offered, then John the Baptist could have fulfilled the prophecies concerning Elijah (v. 14), who was to usher in the day of the Lord (Mal. 4:5). John himself said he was not the resurrected Elijah or the embodiment of his spirit (John 1:21), and the rejection of Jesus and the delay of the establishment of His kingdom on earth made it impossible for John to fulfill all that was predicted of Elijah.

3. *Reaction to John and Jesus* (11:16-19). After paying His tribute to John, Jesus commented briefly on criticism of John and Himself. He compared the Jews of that day to children in a marketplace trying to decide what game to play. First some of them proposed that they play marriage and began piping on musical instruments, but the rest were ornery and would have no part of it. Then the little pipers changed the game to a funeral march and began to make mournful sounds, but the rest would have none of that either. Just so, response to John was criticism for too great austerity or asceticism (he did not want to play wedding) and response to Jesus was condemnation for neglect of Pharisaic exclusiveness and ceremonial fasting (he did not want to play funeral). "But wisdom is proved right by her actions" (NIV); divine wisdom, the plan or method of each man was proved right by the results.

B. Condemnation and Commendation (11:20-30)

1. *Condemnation for unbelief of cities* (11:20-24). It is clear from this passage that neither the performance of miracles nor the very presence of the wonder-working Christ will necessarily lead to mass conversions. The hardness of human hearts and the efforts of Satan to prevent unbelievers from accepting the truth often keep our ministry from being successful. The fault does not always lie in our lack of spiritual power, dedication, or wisdom in carrying on our ministry.

Verses 16-19 show the rejection of Christ and His forerunner by the Jews generally, especially by certain favored cities. Chorazin is about two and one-half miles north of Capernaum at the north end of the Sea of Galilee, and Bethsaida Julias was a couple of miles southeast of Chorazin on the northeast shore of the Sea. There is no record of miracles in either Chorazin or Bethsaida, though the feeding of the 5,000 took place near the latter. The towns were close together and the people of one would be familiar with what went on in the others. Moreover, evidently the Seventy performed miracles in these towns and rejection of the apostles was tantamount to rejection of Christ (Luke 10:12-16).

"Sackcloth and ashes" was the common Eastern way of demonstrating grief. The greater spiritual advantages enjoyed by these two towns would render them doubly guilty at the judgment. Capernaum, which enjoyed the greatest opportunities of all to know the truth and the Person who embodied it, will be most severely judged—with a fate worse than that of Sodom. Greater opportunity to know the truth brings greater responsibility to act on it.

2. *Jesus' thanksgiving and invitation* (11:25-30). In contrast to the condemnation heaped on the spiritually blind inhabitants of three Galilean towns, Jesus rejoiced in the receptivity of some individuals and issued a gracious invitation. "At that time" apparently refers to the return of the Seventy after their ministry (Luke 10:21) and possibly to the return of the Twelve as well. "Jesus answered," responded not to a question but to a situation—to the ways in which His messianic claim was being received. For His part He would "confess openly" or "utter aloud" His praise to the Father in the presence of all.

The "wise and learned" (NIV, scribes and Pharisees and others of the same mind set) find the truth of God withheld from them because they believe it can be known by human reason and effort; and they have so filled their heads with their own pet wisdom about spiritual matters that God can give them nothing further. "Babes" or infants are those who recognize their spiritual helplessness and have a childlike eagerness for the truth of God. Such are in a position to receive "these things," the truth about Jesus' messiahship.

It was God's "good pleasure" to function in this way. His grace is bestowed on those who recognize their need of it, not on those who do not sense their need or who want to come to God on their own terms. Even on the human plane we are disposed to help those who come to us with a sense of inability to solve their own problems; we really cannot do much for those who evidently need help but do not know it and who will not accept it when we offer it.

"All things have been committed to me by my Father" (NIV). "All things" involves an absolutely comprehensive bestowal and implies Christ's deity because the Father would not entrust a mere man with all things. Likewise it implies His humanity because one who was only God would not receive them from another. The mutual knowledge of the Father and the Son is perfect.

In view of the fact that the Father has entrusted the Son with all things—certainly involving the impartation of salvation from sin—Jesus issues an invitation: "Come to me." All who like beasts of burden are weary from all their efforts to live up to the requirements of an elaborate legalism can find spiritual rest by coming to Him. "Take my yoke upon you, and learn from me" is a Jewish figure of speech for discipline and discipleship. It is equivalent to saying "Become my disciples."

"For I am gentle and humble in heart" (NIV) perhaps has a double significance: He will be gracious and mild in dealing with those who come as little children; and He Himself had learned the way of complete obedience and subjection to the Father (Phil. 2:1-8; Heb. 10:7,9). "Rest for your souls" will come when the load of sin is lifted and spiritual life is imparted. "My burden is light"—"That rest which the soul experiences, when once safe under Christ's wing, makes all yokes easy, all burdens light" (Brown, p. 68).

C. Confrontation With the Pharisees (12:1-45)

1. *Sabbath-breaking question* (12:1-14). Matthew next introduces a series of incidents to show the hostility of the Pharisees. This antipathy, introduced in 9:11,34, reached new heights (v. 14). The Pharisees' first clash with Jesus was over Sabbath breaking. "At that season" may refer to the harvest season, to an indefinite time, or to the same time as indicated in 11:25. Perhaps as the disciples walked to or from the synagogue on the Sabbath, they passed some ripened grain in the fields. Being very hungry, they picked a few handfuls of grain and ate them. The grain was not corn, as some versions translate, because corn was not grown in Palestine until after the Spanish discovery of America. It was either barley or wheat, probably the latter.

The Pharisees, looking for a case against Jesus, pounced as the disciples "began to pick" the grain. Evidently Jesus had picked none, for only the disciples were accused of Sabbath breaking. The accusation of the Pharisees was not that the disciples were breaking the Sabbath by going for a long walk in the fields. In fact, the Pharisees themselves observed the activity of the disciples. Therefore, the fields must have been right on the edge of town and easily accessible from the road. Moreover, the disciples were not accused of stealing; the law permitted one to pick a little grain in his neighbor's field for his personal use (Deut.

23:25). Rather, the charge centered on a rabbinical interpretation that any picking of grain on the Sabbath was a form of reaping and thus a breaking of the Sabbath (Exod. 20:10).

Jesus responded with a series of biblical observations. David, when he was hungry, obtained from Ahimelech the priest five loaves of consecrated bread from the tabernacle at Nob—bread which only priests could lawfully eat (1 Sam. 21:1-7; cf. Exod. 25:23-30; Lev. 24:5-9). "Have you not read" is tantamount to saying, Have you "not grasped the spiritual principle set forth . . . , that human necessity must take precedence over legal technicalities?" (Tasker, p. 124)

A second biblical observation (vv. 5-6) involved the fact that the priests themselves were required to work on the Sabbath and so to break the law; thus the Sabbath law was not absolute (Num. 28:9-10). In observing that priests in the temple had to break the Sabbath law in performing their tasks, Jesus declared that He was "greater than the temple." "With His coming the Temple and all that it stood for is in fact superseded. The Temple was believed to enshrine the divine presence, but in Jesus, the Messiah, the divine presence is incarnate" (Tasker, p. 125).

Jesus made yet a third point from the Scripture. The Pharisees had failed to grasp the truth of Hosea 6:6, that God desires right hearts more than external formalities; and therefore they had condemned "innocent ones." Jesus pronounced the disciples "guiltless," and He had the right to do so because He was "Lord of the Sabbath." He had instituted the Sabbath and, as Lord of it, He knew what Sabbath law involved, when it was being violated, and when it was being perverted by the likes of the Pharisees.

Further attack of the Pharisees on Jesus occurred in connection with a case of healing in the synagogue. From Matthew this event could be construed as coming on the same Sabbath; Luke 6:6-11 shows that it was on another Sabbath. A man with a paralyzed or shriveled hand was there. The Pharisees, trying to trap Jesus, asked Him only whether it was lawful to heal on the Sabbath. In the event of an emergency, there would have been no question. Clearly this was no emergency; the disabled one could have waited until nightfall. But Jesus was disgusted with their callous attitude. "Any one" who had a sheep fall into a pit on the Sabbath would scurry around and get it out—to say nothing of what he would do for a whole flock. Of course a man is worth infinitely more than a sheep; to withhold aid is to do evil. Declaring that it was lawful to do good on the Sabbath, Jesus healed the man completely. Enraged, the Pharisees went out to plot the death of Jesus. Men who viewed healing on the Sabbath a violation of that holy day had no compunction about plotting murder on the Sabbath.

2. *Jesus' avoidance of publicity* (12:15-21). Aware of this plot, Jesus withdrew for ministry elsewhere. He was not afraid but He was after all operating according to a divine timetable. His hour for bearing the sin of the world as an infinite sacrifice had not yet come. And He had much work left to do, especially in training disciples and preparing them to carry on His unfinished task. As He ministered to the crowds, He "healed all their sick" but urged that His miracles not be used as a means to advertise Him as Messiah and thus to excite the crowd and increase the opposition.

This ministry of Jesus and the manner of it is viewed as fulfillment of prophecy. Verse 17 is a claim to inspiration: God Himself spoke through His instrument, the "prophet Isaiah." The verse also gives support to Isaiah's authorship of the latter half of the book that bears his name, a position commonly denied by liberal critics. This support is seen in the fact that the quotation attributed to Isaiah comes from Isaiah 42:1-4. This passage portrays the spiritual aspects of Messiah's kingdom in contrast to the political character anticipated by Jews in general and the disciples in particular.

Clearly verse 18 teaches that Jesus Christ, not the nation Israel (as modern Jews often claim), was in view in Isaiah's prophecies of the Servant of the Lord. Moreover, the verse sets forth Messiah's relation to the Sender, His enablement for His task (the Holy Spirit), and His mission: "to announce right to the Gentiles." Lenski interprets "right" to be "the gospel verdict which conveys 'righteousness,' . . . the acquittal of pardon through God's grace. Back of it lies redemption" (p. 473).

The Messiah will carry on His mission in a nonviolent manner, with no loud proclamations such as might be expected from an earthly prince (v. 19) and with gentleness (v. 20). The "bruised reed" and "feebly burning wick," those spiritually feeble and virtually destroyed by sin, He will restore. "Till He has made justice victorious" (Beck) envisions the grandeur and completeness of Messiah's victories. Messiah's ministry will not be restricted to the Jews: "His name will be the hope of the nations" (Beck). The Gentiles will find that nothing in the world can save them but faith in Christ.

3. *The Beelzebub controversy* (12:22-37). Next comes a dramatic

shift from a true characterization of Jesus by divine inspiration to a vindictive characterization by the Pharisees. Setting the stage for this Pharisaic slander is a brief account of Jesus' restoration of a man afflicted with demon possession, which had resulted in blindness and dumbness. The response of lay bystanders was one of astonishment: "This cannot be the Son of David, can he?" The question implies a negative answer, for they can hardly entertain such a marvelous thought. But hope is implied.

The Pharisees sought to blast such a hope with the vicious accusation that Jesus could control demons because He was in league with Beelzebul (Beelzebub), or Satan, the prince of demons. "This fellow" is a very derogatory descriptive and "only" implies that He has no power of His own to expel demons but must do it only in league with Satan.

Evidently the Pharisees did not level this charge in Jesus' presence because He is represented as "knowing their thoughts." Then Jesus uttered a truism, that every kingdom or city or household that has one faction fighting against another will be devastated by a common enemy. Apparently Jesus had in mind warfare between Satan's kingdom and the kingdom of God. If Satan acted through demons or henchmen such as Jesus in driving out demons, actually he would be engaged in fighting against himself; and his kingdom would not be able to stand in any conflict with the kingdom of God.

"By whom do your sons [disciples] drive them out?" These disciples either had the power or claimed to have the power of exorcism and of course believed that such power came from God. How ridiculous to assert that the identical exercise of power in Jesus came from satanic inspiration when, as Jesus had just shown, such a claim is self-contradictory! "They shall be your judges"; the disciples of the Pharisees will expose or condemn their masters on this point. And if Jesus drove out demons by the power of the Holy Spirit instead of an evil spirit, that would be proof of the arrival of God's kingdom among them—of the presence of the divine rule which can defeat Satan.

To strengthen His case further, Jesus set forth another parabolic thought in verse 29. The interpretation and application is that Jesus could not enter Satan's dominion and free the deaf and dumb demoniac until He had first subdued Satan himself. Then He could bring release to the demoniac.

There is no neutral ground in the conflict between God and Satan. To stand in the way of acceptance of Jesus as King, as the Pharisees were doing, was to "scatter" those who otherwise would be candidates for membership in the kingdom. The Pharisees were on Satan's side—knowingly so—and were therefore guilty of an unpardonable sin. "Every other kind of sin" will be forgiven, except blasphemy against the Holy Spirit. This blasphemy consists in adamantly setting oneself against Christ and attributing to satanic power that which He did in the power of the Holy Spirit.

Viewed strictly historically, this sin could be committed only when Jesus was physically present and therefore has no relevance for the present (see Mark 3:29-30). Viewed more generally, it may refer to opposition to God that has become so fierce and so fixed as to remove the individual from the gracious wooing of the Holy Spirit. One who has reached such a point of no return can expect no forgiveness "in this age, or in the age to come." Clearly this is a solemn warning; if the Pharisees had not yet fully reached this irreversible state, they were in danger of doing so.

In verses 33-37 Jesus compares His works with those of the Pharisees. "A tree is recognized by its fruit" (NIV); its fruit is consistent with its nature. Carr properly represents Jesus as requesting, "Either say that I am evil and that my works are evil, or, if you admit that my works are good, admit that I am good also and not in league with Beelzebub" (p. 182). Then turning the argument against them, He says, in effect, "Your words and actions are evil and rise from an evil source." Jesus hurled a scurrilous condemnation against the Pharisees as John the Baptist had earlier (3:7): "Brood of vipers," descendants from the Serpent himself (John 8:44), who are "evil," actively, viciously wicked; nothing "good" can come out of your mouths.

Then Jesus used two figures—the reservoir and treasury. The heart like a reservoir overflows in speech; and when the occasion arises an individual draws on the thoughts and judgments he has stored up. Lenski aptly observes: "When they claimed that his expelling the demons proved his connection with Satan they revealed only with what their wicked hearts were overflowing. . . , real devil's thoughts" (p. 487). The Pharisees had, after all, already resolved to destroy Jesus (Matt. 12:14).

If speech is a guide to true character or spiritual condition, then men are to be judged by their words as much as by their works on the Day of Judgment. What comes out of a person's mouth in a moment of pressure, of sorrow, or of joy is some guide to his true spiritual condition. But God is the only omniscient judge; He alone understands motives, true spiritual condition, and the character of our words and works. Men must be careful not to set themselves up as God in the lives of others. Any judgments that we are forced to make in carrying on our ministry must be made in humility and with tentativeness.

4. *The demand for a sign* (12:38-45). Matthew's placement of this request, as in the parallel passage in Luke 11:29-44, leaves the impression that it came about the same time as the Pharisees' accusation that Jesus cast out demons by the power of Satan. If so, it is impudent and hypocritical. They had witnessed many miracles during His ministry in Galilee; the latest one they had attributed to satanic power. What kind of miracle they wanted now is not clear. The demand seems almost to be a taunting: "If you are really the Messiah, prove it by something so spectacular that there will be no doubt in our minds." If they were asking for a sign from heaven (Matt. 16:1), one not originated by Jesus, then Jesus said that ultimately they would have such a sign, but none would be given them then.

But even when the sign of the Resurrection was given, the Pharisees did their best to deny it or explain it away. The miracle which supremely demonstrated that Jesus was the Son of God was the Resurrection, and Jonah's temporary living death in the belly of the great fish was viewed as prefiguring Christ's burial in the earth. The people of Nineveh on the Judgment Day will put to shame the Jews of Jesus' generation, for by their penitence they will condemn the impenitent Jews. Jesus in His messianic ministry far transcended Jonah's preaching of repentance to a heathen city or the wisdom of Solomon, which attracted the Queen of Sheba to come some 1200 miles to bask in his brilliance.

Then Jesus concluded with a parable that pictured the spiritual condition of "this generation" of Jews. They were like a man who had had an evil spirit expelled from his life; his house now stood empty, "swept clean and put in order" (NIV) and waiting for a new occupant. The ministry of John the Baptist and Jesus had resulted in a kind of moral cleansing. But in most cases the houses stood empty: Jesus had not been invited in to live there. So the devil who had been expelled viewed this vacuum to be an attractive and available lodging and brought seven other demons to live there with him, with the result that the man's latter state was worse than his former one. The degree of degradation of some of the Jews is revealed in their attitude toward Jesus in this chapter, culminating in the blasphemy against the Holy Spirit. This continuing spiritual decline and the judgment on them for it eventuated in the destruction of Jerusalem in A.D. 70.

D. Interference of Relatives (12:46-50)

While Jesus was still talking to the people, His "mother and brothers" arrived from Nazareth (cf. Mark 3:31-35). Since Joseph is not mentioned, presumably he was no longer living; the "brothers" are most naturally understood to be younger sons of Mary and Joseph. Apparently they had come to take Jesus away from His ministry for rest and recuperation and possibly for protection against His enemies.

"Standing outside" either the house or the throng He was addressing, Jesus' family sent in a message asking Him to come out and speak with them. But He refused to allow His relatives to interfere with His ministry. Then gesturing toward His disciples, He said that they were His new spiritual family: His "mother and brothers." Since the disciples were all men, evidently He was speaking of something higher than blood ties. Presumably father is not included with family members because Christ reserved reference to a father to the heavenly Father. "Whoever does the will of my Father in heaven," whoever hears and believes and follows God's Son, is a member of My new spiritual family. There is no indication whether Jesus' relatives ever did manage to talk with Him on this occasion. Probably He did not snub them entirely, but certainly He did not allow them to interrupt His ministry.

For Further Study

1. Try to discover four characteristics that made John the Baptist effective or great.

2. Bethsaida, Chorazin, and Capernaum no longer exist. From Bible dictionaries or encyclopedias try to learn something of the history and archaeology of these places which came under the curse of Jesus (11:20-24).

3. Locate three good examples of the gentleness of Jesus (Matt. 11:28).

4. Is there any evidence that Jesus ever broke the Sabbath or any other Mosaic law as His enemies accused Him of doing?

Chapter 8

Parables of the Messiah's Kingdom
(Matthew 13:1-52)

A. Preliminaries to the Parables (13:1-2,10-17)

1. *Speaking in parables* (13:1-2). Later, on the "same day" as the Beelzebub confrontation and the visit of Jesus' relatives, He delivered a series of kingdom parables. The crowd grew so vast and pressed in on Him so eagerly that He decided it was best to use a fishing boat as a pulpit and to speak to them from a few feet out in the water. "The boat" is the same one He used on other occasions; it evidently belonged to Peter. On this occasion He spoke in "parables." A parable is a comparison or analogy drawn from daily life or nature and used to impart or enforce a spiritual truth. These short fictitious narratives about some human experience well known to the hearer were plausible occurrences in the lives of those to whom they were addressed.

2. *Reason for speaking in parables* (13:10-17). Many modern disciples ask why Jesus spoke in parables, just as did the original Twelve (v. 10). Jesus answered rather pointedly: "The knowledge of the secrets of the kingdom of heaven has been given to you, but not to them" (NIV). This "knowledge" "has been given"; it has been revealed by God Himself to members of the inner circle, not to outsiders. This is not unjust or wrong. It has always been true that some secrets are reserved for insiders, for the family, whether the family be a small group with blood ties, members of a club, of a corporation, or a religious order. One does not discuss with strangers or enemies the intimate concerns that might be appreciated only by friends. Jesus Himself said on another occasion that His obedient disciples, as friends, would be the recipients of a deeper understanding of spiritual things (John 15:15).

Sometimes it is charged that Jesus was unfair in hiding the truth to prevent some from understanding it and becoming converted (v. 15; cf. Mark 4:11-12). It should be noted, however, that the spiritually responsive were never denied the truth; the invitation to receive Christ was always open, clear, and uncomplicated. It was those who had hardened their hearts against Christ who were being dealt with in parables on this occasion. Many in the crowd had just committed the unpardonable sin; they had hardened their hearts so long and had fiercely opposed Christ so often that He had given them up, and judgment had fallen in the withdrawal of further opportunity to repent. But even though Jesus sometimes spoke in parables to the Pharisees, the truth was not completely veiled; they generally got the point of what He was trying to say and frequently winced under His stinging attacks (e.g., Matt. 21:45). What is being veiled in Matthew 13 is not so much the converting message of the kingdom as the "secrets" or inner workings of the kingdom.

The somewhat enigmatic phraseology of verse 12 is not difficult to interpret. "Whoever has" willingly accepted the truth given will receive more—in abundance. "Whoever does not have," does not possess any truth because he has refused to accept what was offered him, "what he has will be taken away"; he may even lose any sense of fairness and justice. Certainly this was true of the Pharisees, for they became increasingly perverted in their attitude toward Jesus, even accusing Him of performing miracles by the power of Satan and plotting to kill Him for doing good.

Though many had seen and heard the magnificent works of Christ, they did not appropriate the truth but turned against it. Therefore He spoke to them in parables and thus withheld from them some truths of the kingdom in a beginning act of judgment. God's Spirit will not always strive with men (Gen. 6:3).

In His free quotation of Isaiah 6:9-10, Jesus in effect was stating that Isaiah's prophecy "is being fulfilled" at least partially in the state of spiritual insensitivity that was settling on many of Jesus' hearers. Their heart "has become calloused" (NIV), they became almost deaf to the truth, they deliberately shut their eyes, and they were determined not to make an about face or be converted ("lest they should see," "hear," "understand," "turn"). In marked contrast, the disciples "see" and "hear" and have received the Messiah. Thus they enjoyed the marvelous privileges anticipated by the prophets and righteous men throughout the Old Testament period.

B. Preaching the Parables (13:3-9,18-52)

1. *The sower parable* (13:3-9,18-23). In the days before the invention of the seed drill (about 1701), a farmer scattered his seed on top of the ground at sowing time. Some of it was lost because it fell around the edges of the field, on hard or stony ground, or in weedbeds. Jesus used this familiar experience of His hearers to serve as a vehicle for teaching spiritual truth. Seed falling on a hard footpath or a road lay exposed where birds could eat it. Seed falling on a thin layer of soil covering rocks might germinate quickly but then die under the scorching rays of a Palestinian sun because there was no subsoil into which it could send its roots for moisture. Seed landing among thorns and other weeds commonly produced puny plants and no fruit because the thorns grew faster than barley or wheat and made it difficult for good seed to produce. Of course most of the seed landed on good soil, where it had varying degrees of yield. The seed was of equally good quality; problems of germination and fruitbearing lay in the soil.

Fortunately, for the sower parable there is an inspired interpretation. Though the sower is not identified, he evidently represents Christ or others who preach the gospel. The seed stands for the Word of God. And the four soils represent four attitudes toward the Word on the part of hearers. In the case of the first type of soil, the birds represent Satan who comes and snatches away the seed before it has a chance to germinate. Thin soil above a rocky substratum represents individuals who with enthusiasm or emotional fervor are temporary adherents to the truth; but it never permeates beyond a superficial level in their lives. Seed falling among thorns does germinate and sends down its roots, but the plant is so choked by hindrances to growth that it bears no fruit. These hindrances are described as distracting anxieties that almost literally cut a person to pieces and the deceptive nature of wealth which promises to satisfy and never does.

The good soil speaks of those who hear or accept the Word, continue to appropriate it, and continue to bear fruit. The greater the degree of hearing and appropriating of the Word, the greater the degree of fruitbearing. Thus this parable describes the various responses to Christ's message as He preached it and responses to the gospel during this present age as the message of Christ is preached.

2. *Parable of the wheat and tares* (13:24-30,36-43). The kingdom of heaven is next compared to a man with the following experience. He

sowed good seed in his field. During the night his enemy came and "sowed over" the ground with tares and slipped away. "Tares" evidently are darnel, a weed that in its early stages of growth closely resembles wheat. This similarity gives point to the parable, for in professing Christendom it is not always possible to distinguish true believers from the counterfeit. As growth takes place, however, it finally becomes evident that the field of grain has a large amount of darnel in it—too much to have blown in by chance. The farmhands of the owner raise a question about his own action in planting the field. He declares an enemy is responsible for the deplorable situation; he is not guilty of carelessness. Cases of such spiteful action have occurred in the Near East even in modern times.

The laborers then ask whether they should try to clear out the darnel. But the owner observes that that would be a mistake because in the process they might "root up" the wheat. If wheat and darnel are allowed to grow together until harvest time, it will be abundantly evident which is the true wheat and no mistakes will be made. "By their fruits ye shall know them" (Matt. 7:20).

Though Jesus probably delivered all the parables of Matthew 13 on the same day, He did not work them into His conversation one after the other. There were breaks in the activity of the day when the disciples could ask about interpretation (vv. 10, 36). As in the case of the sower parable, so in case of the wheat and tares, Jesus offered an authoritative interpretation. The field is declared to be "the world," not the church. In the church heretics and other offenders are to be disciplined (Matt. 18:15-19; 1 Cor. 5). The "good seed" are "sons of the kingdom," not the word, as in the sower parable. The tares are the "sons of the wicked one," Christ rejecters who the devil has planted alongside true believers.

The focus is not on good seed and evil seed because all persons are sinners and bound for eternal punishment before some accept Christ as their Savior. Rather, the parable teaches that in society there are true believers alongside whom appear outwardly good persons who are spiritually dead. While society and the church may uproot outwardly evil persons, they are to keep hands off outwardly good persons who may not be believers at all. God looks on the heart and He alone should be allowed to execute judgment on such persons through the action of His angels.

At the time of "harvest" or judgment, at the "end of the age," the angels will gather out such darnel or counterfeits and send them to perdition (the "furnace of fire," cf. Matt. 25:41; Mark 9:44; Rev. 19:20; 21:8). Living believers will remain to live "in the kingdom of their Father," evidently the millennial age. The judgment is parallel to that portrayed in Matthew 25:31-36. There is no reference here to resurrection of either the wicked or righteous dead; evidently neither a general judgment nor the final judgment is in view. Of course, true believers and counterfeits who die before the final generation of the present age will be sorted out at death.

3. *Mustard seed parable* (13:31-32). The kingdom of heaven is next compared to a mustard seed (the Word), which a man (probably Christ) sowed in his field (probably the world, cf. v. 38). The mustard is not "the least of all seeds" (KJV) but comparatively "smaller" than the other seeds to be found in an herb garden; smaller seeds are known. The Palestinian mustard seed is black and very tiny, like a petunia seed. It produces a tree-sized plant twelve to fourteen feet or more in height. Though the parable is not interpreted, its meaning is evident. The kingdom had a very insignificant beginning but grew to be startlingly large, dwarfing all other plants in the garden (perhaps all other religious systems in significance). Birds—not part of the kingdom—find shelter in the tree and enjoy the beneficial influences of the kingdom in the world.

4. *Parable of the leaven* (13:33-35). It is common to interpret the parable of the leaven as portraying the spreading influence of the gospel in the world. As leaven or yeast permeates all the dough into which it is inserted, so the gospel is to permeate the world. But leaven standardly symbolizes evil in Scripture; in the fermentation process it is decomposing and destructive. Jesus used this symbol to refer to the evil teachings of the Pharisees, Sadducees, and Herod (Matt. 16:6-12). If leaven is to represent beneficent powers here, it is the single instance where it speaks of something good.

It seems best to maintain biblical consistency and to see here a warning that false doctrine would infiltrate the kingdom. Evil action is present throughout the parables already uttered. Birds representing Satan snatch away the seed in the parable of the sower; the evil one deliberately plants darnel or counterfeits alongside true sons of the kingdom; birds (probably evil ones) nest in the mustard tree (v. 32); and here a woman deliberately and with specific intention mixes yeast into the flour. A "man" is not doing the mixing here as a man sowed wheat or mustard; apparently someone other than Christ is active in this case.

Perhaps this "woman" is to be compared with "that woman Jezebel" (Rev. 2:20) or the "great harlot" (Rev. 17:5) as an opponent of Christ and true doctrine.

The first four parables Jesus spoke publicly to the crowd gathered around Him (v. 34), and apparently He did not interpret the message of any of them. Since He here dismissed the crowd and went into a house with His disciples where He interpreted the parable of the wheat and tares (v. 36), it may be concluded that the last three parables were given privately to the disciples. The parabolic preaching is seen as a fulfillment of the prophet's function (v. 35; cf. Ps. 78:2).

5. *Parable of the hid treasure and pearl* (13:44-46). Commonly these two closely related parables are viewed as exhorting a sinner to give up all worldly pleasures and attainments, to sell all, in order to find the pearl or treasure: salvation. But the field in these parables must represent the world, as it does in the first two parables of Matthew 13. It is quite incongruous for a sinner to give up the world and its allurements and then to turn around and buy the world in order to gain salvation, which is a treasure hidden in the world. That is not the gospel. The sinner is destitute, having nothing to offer in gaining salvation. The gospel is the grace of God making provision for the sinner and seeking him in his sin.

The man who gave up all to buy the field or treasure and the merchant who bought the pearl can be none other than Christ who gave His life to pay the sin-debt of the whole world. Within the world of sinners are those who believe on Him—treasure and pearl. Some see the treasure as representative of Israel and the pearl as the church. Others view the treasure as portraying believers individually and the pearl as portraying them collectively. It is difficult to identify the treasure and pearl certainly, but the main point of the parables seems clear: the value of believers to Christ who made the supreme sacrifice for them.

6. *Parable of the net* (13:47-52). The message of this parable is similar to that of the wheat and tares. The kingdom, like a huge fishnet, will come to envelop all kinds of people ("fish"), some genuinely converted and others making an empty profession. These may all swim around together for as long as the net is allowed to remain in the water. But ultimately the fisherman comes to take in the net and determine which fish are useful to him. He tosses out the rejects. Just so at the judgment "at the end of the age" the bad fish or the wicked will be

separated out and sent into "the fiery furnace" of judgment (cf. vv. 30, 42). Presumably the good remain and go into the millennial kingdom as was true in verse 43.

At the conclusion of this parable, the disciples indicate their understanding of the points Jesus has been making in His parables. Then He responds by comparing them as informed teachers of God's truth to a householder with a full storeroom for the conduct of his tasks. "Things new and old" refers to the truths of the Old Testament and new truths of the kingdom, such as those revealed in these parables.

For Further Study

1. With the help of a concordance and a commentary, study the references to leaven in Scripture, with emphasis on the New Testament.

2. To see somewhat differing interpretations of these parables, consult A. M. Hunter, *Interpreting the Parables;* G. Campbell Morgan, *The Parables and Metaphors of Our Lord;* and Richard C. Trench, *Notes on the Parables of Our Lord.*

3. Try to locate examples of parables that Jesus used to promote understanding or communicate truth rather than to hide the deeper truths of the kingdom.

Chapter 9

Messiah's Withdrawals From Galilee

(Matthew 13:53–18:35)

Jesus' final rejection at Nazareth, the report of John the Baptist's murder, and Herod's response to Jesus' ministry served as the occasion for the Master's first withdrawal from Galilee (Herod's domain). During subsequent weeks, until departure for Jerusalem, He concentrated His attention on training the disciples. This training related especially to a total of three withdrawals from Galilee (to the eastern shore of the Sea of Galilee, north to the region of Tyre and Sidon, and northeast to the vicinity of Caesarea Philippi and the Mount of Transfiguration) and a session in Capernaum upon return.

A. First Withdrawal and the First Multiplication of the Loaves (13:53–14:36)

1. *Rejection at Nazareth* (13:53-58). At the beginning of Jesus' ministry in Galilee (4:12), He had been rejected at Nazareth and had left under the threat of assassination. Now, near the end of His Galilean ministry, He returned to Nazareth and again suffered rejection. As He "began to teach in their synagogue," they were "dumbfounded" and wondered where He had gotten His wisdom and miraculous powers. When He left Nazareth, He was not renowned as a miracle worker and they could not figure Him out. They thought they knew all there was to know about Him. After all, He had grown up among them. He was "the carpenter's son"; in fact, He had evidently taken over the family business, for Mark 6:3 calls Him "the carpenter" in a parallel passage. Since Joseph nowhere figures in this narrative, he is presumed dead by this time. Moreover, the synagogue hearers knew Jesus' mother and His brothers and His sisters, who must have been married and living in the

Nazareth area—"with us." Of the four brothers named, James later became head of the church in Jerusalem and the writer of an epistle, and Jude (Judas) is commonly identified as the writer of the epistle that bears his name. Nothing further is known of Joseph and Simon. The most natural way to interpret New Testament statements about the brothers and sisters of Jesus is to consider them as natural children of Joseph and Mary, born after Jesus—"the firstborn." Some try to make out a case for the view that they were cousins of Jesus or sons of Joseph by a previous marriage—thus preserving the perpetual virginity of Mary.

The Nazareth crowd could not figure out where Jesus got "all these things"; He was functioning as a learned rabbi but had been reared and had worked as a carpenter. Thus they could not bring themselves to the belief that His wisdom and works were of divine origin: they found in Him a cause of stumbling and "they turned against Him" (v. 57 Beck). Jesus replied with a proverb often used in the ancient world. This observation involved a claim to the prophetic office and shows clearly the main function of a prophet—to proclaim truth rather than to predict the future. Evidently Jesus had not been predicting the future and rarely would do so later on. "He did not do many miracles there because of their unbelief." Their prejudice against Him hindered belief, and Jesus did not use miraculous works to induce faith in those adamantly set against Him.

2. *Herod's troubled conscience* (14:1-12). "At that time," the time of growing hostility to Jesus, "Herod the tetrarch" heard of Jesus' fame. This was Herod Antipas, tetrarch of Galilee and Perea (the area east of the Jordan River). A son of Herod the Great and Malthace, a Samaritan, Antipas had been brought up in Rome with his brother Archelaus. Herod's first wife was a daughter of Aretas, king of Arabia; and while still married to her, he married Herodias, the wife of his half-brother Philip (not Philip the tetrarch who ruled the area northeast of the Sea of Galilee). This sin had brought on the denunciation of John the Baptist and Herodias's inveterate hatred of John and her determination to dispose of him.

"Tetrarch" is literally the ruler of a fourth part or district of a province, but the name came to denote a petty king. "King" (v. 9) also may be viewed as merely a courtesy title. Herod's conscience was still so troubled over his murder of John that word of Jesus' remarkable powers led his clouded brain to conclude that Jesus was John resurrected.

Verses 3-12 are parenthetical and flash back to the story of John's execution in an effort to explain Herod's troubled conscience (cf. Mark 6:14-29; Luke 9:7-9). Several aspects of Herod's treatment of John stand out clearly in this account. First, his animosity toward John was not so much personal as it was prompted by Herodias ("because of Herodias" NIV). Second, though Herodias urged Herod to execute John, he was deterred by John's popular support. Third, Herod's birthday party became the occasion of John's death. During the celebration, Salome, Herodias's daughter, danced for the all-male gathering of dignitaries. Normally this was something a slave girl rather than a princess would do. Evidently her erotic performance excited the half-drunk Herod and won a rash promise of generous proportions. Herodias took advantage of the situation to prompt her daughter to ask for the head of John the Baptist. Fourth, Herod was outclassed by a scheming, callous wife and an equally callous stepdaughter. Fifth, having given his oath before all the members of his political and social circle, he could not renege; he gave the order for John's immediate execution.

3. *Jesus' first withdrawal* (14:13-14). "When Jesus heard this, he withdrew." The most natural interpretation seems to be that when Jesus heard about John's murder, He withdrew. For a fuller explanation, it is necessary to turn to Mark 6:30, where it is indicated that Jesus wanted to confer in private with His disciples who were just returning from a missionary tour of Galilee. This, then, would be a debriefing session. And in this context the discussion no doubt also included some reflection on the cost of discipleship. It is also possible, of course, to interpret "this" in verse 13 as referring to Jesus' hearing of Herod's estimation of His own ministry. Aware of the rising opposition to Him, Jesus would henceforth spend increasing amounts of time with His disciples, preparing them for the ministry they must perform after His departure.

Jesus retired to an "uninhabited place," where the apostolic company could be alone. Their destination was the vicinity of Bethsaida, on the northeast shore of the Sea of Galilee, not a "desert" region in the sense that it was barren of foliage. Traveling by boat, they apparently arrived before the crowds who went on foot around the northern shore of the sea. Evidently Jesus spent a while with the disciples before facing the crowds (cf. John 6:3-5). The translation "when he came out" (v. 14 NASB) is closer to the original than many other modern versions and seems to indicate that Jesus came out of some secluded spot rather than out of a boat. The great heart of Jesus was moved as He saw the crowd of

sick ones—literally, those without strength—who had been transported such a great distance; and He healed them.

4. *First multiplication of loaves* (14:15-21). The feeding of the
5,000 is the only one of the thirty-five specifically mentioned miracles of
Jesus to be recorded in all four Gospels. The Gospel of John alludes to
the fact that Jesus had been concerned about feeding the crowd from the
very first moment He had encountered them. He had inquired of Philip
where food could be bought for such a multitude, but "he asked this only
to test him, for he already had in mind what he was going to do" (6:6 NIV).

Philip's response demonstrated the impossibility of coming up with
enough money to make the purchase. For some hours Philip had turned
over Jesus' question in his mind, but he had developed no new insights.
No doubt other disciples also had thought about the problem. Finally,
"as evening approached," the disciples came in a body and urged Jesus
to send the people away to buy themselves food. In order to test them
Jesus observed, "They do not need to go away. You give them something
to eat" (NIV). On investigation they found a small boy with five flat barley
cakes and two small fish (John 6:9).

Jesus had been trying to lead the disciples to suggest miraculous
provision. When they did not, He took the initiative and prepared for
the miracle. He directed the people to sit on the grass (it was Passover
time, in the spring when all was green). Then, after prayer, He multiplied the cakes and the fish and the disciples acted as waiters. "All ate"
and ate all they wanted—"were satiated" or "filled." And there were
twelve basketfuls left over—twelve baskets of the type travelers used to
carry food and other necessities. There was one for each of the disciples.
The number fed was 5,000 men besides women and children; so the total
could have reached 10,000 or more. That this figure is not a loose
estimate is arrived at from the fact that the crowd sat down in groups of
fifties and hundreds (Mark 6:39-40).

5. *Miracle on the sea* (14:22-33). As soon as the crowd was fed,
"Jesus made the disciples get into the boat." Evidently "the boat" was
the one so often used by the disciples; it was no doubt the property of
Peter and Andrew. The reason for this hasty action was the plan of the
crowd to take Jesus by force and make Him King (John 6:15). Probably
the disciples would have been very happy to participate in such an
action; so Jesus separated them from the crowd. Then He dismissed the
crowd and went up on a hillside to pray. His need for prayer was evident
in view of the temptation to swerve from a course of action that would

make Him the Sin-Bearer of the world and the anticipation of defection
of many of His followers the next day (John 6:22,66-71).

After the disciples sailed for the western shore of the Sea of Galilee,
one of the treacherous and unexpected storms for which the sea is
notorious descended on them. It caught them some three and one-half
miles from land (John 6:19); and even after hours of rowing against the
storm, they were able to make no progress. It is significant to note that
the disciples found themselves in great difficulty while they were following the direct command of Christ. Commonly modern believers feel that
dire circumstances must be an indication they are out of the will of God.
Evidently such a conclusion often is unwarranted.

Jesus was not unmindful of the plight of His followers. Just about
the time they must have been at the point of exhaustion, He went into
action. During the fourth watch of the night (three to six A.M.), after
they had been rowing for hours, Jesus went out to them, "walking
on the sea." As He walked there, it is evident that He was Lord of
creation, with power over wind and wave and the forces of gravity.
Thinking they were seeing a ghost, the disciples shrieked aloud.
Lenski explains, "They are shaken because they think that this un-
earthly form walking toward them is a sure sign that they are all doomed
men" (p. 572).

Jesus allays their fears: "It is I. Stop being afraid." In verse 28 Peter
is not asking Jesus to prove His identity. The Greek could just as well be
translated, "Since it is you." Then in an impulse of the moment, Peter
seems to be saying, "I believe in You so thoroughly that if You command
me to walk toward You on the water, I would have the power to do it."
Peter did not appear to be showing off his faith before the others or to be
claiming he had more faith than they; Jesus presumably would not have
honored faith with ulterior motives under these circumstances. Jesus
accepted the expression of faith and issued the command. Peter obeyed
and walked on the water. Likely there was a calm path in the water
between the boat and Jesus or Peter probably would not have ventured
over the side of the boat.

Peter walked away from the security of the planks beneath his feet
and looked at the churning waves around him. As he took his eyes and
his mind off Jesus, the source of the power to perform the act in which he
was engaging, he began to sink. Immediately his faith returned as he
cried for help to the only one capable of meeting his need. The touch of
the Master's hand kept Peter from sinking. "You of little faith": faith in

Jesus as the Messiah should be adequate for even the most demanding challenges of life. Certainly that was why the miracle had been granted in the first place.

When Peter and Jesus climbed into the boat, the storm not only ceased but the boat immediately came to land—immediately was transported over several miles of water (John 6:21). If the boat was only some three and one-half miles from the eastern shore of the sea when Jesus came to them, it would have been only about halfway across the lake. But immediately it was at the Capernaum shore. Such a demonstration of power over the forces of nature brought the disciples to the recognition of Jesus' deity and to the worship of Him: "Truly you are the Son of God." Human beings may exorcise demons and physical healing may be explained away in some naturalistic fashion, but only God could have such control over the forces of nature. Later that day Peter was to verbalize this same confession more fully (John 6:68-69).

6. *Gennesaret healing* (14:34-36). As is made clear from John 6, after the storm at sea Jesus and the disciples landed at Capernaum, where on the next day He delivered the discourse on the Bread of Life and suffered some defection from the ranks of His followers. Evidently during subsequent days Jesus moved south of Capernaum into the Plain of Gennesaret, which extended about three miles along the shore and two miles inland. This seems to have been a territory where He had not ministered before because some of the "men," who may have seen Him in Capernaum or elsewhere, "recognized Him." Going to a locality where He had not been before seems consistent with Jesus' withdrawal from His previous centers of activity, which characterizes this section of the Gospel.

As Jesus moved through Gennesaret, the people of the place brought to Him all their sick (see also Mark 6:53-56). Interestingly, they did not ask Him to lay His hands on their loved ones and heal them but only requested that the suffering ones be allowed to "touch the tassel of His cloak." Presumably this is no evidence of a superstitious belief that miraculous powers resided in His clothing but that all about Him radiated the power of God. The picture is a beautiful one. The Master walked among the sick lying on their pallets on the ground. These helpless ones, unable to stir themselves further, reached out their feeble hands in an act of faith—if only to touch the tassel of His cloak. Their exercise of faith was rewarded and they were "completely cured."

B. Second Withdrawal and the Second Multiplication of the Loaves (15:1-39)

1. *Clash with scribes and Pharisees* (15:1-20). "Then," not necessarily while Jesus was still in Gennesaret, but during that general period of His life, a delegation of scribes and Pharisees arrived from Jerusalem to team up with local opponents of Jesus to harass and discredit Him. They attacked indirectly, censuring His disciples. By implication they were criticizing Him, however, for He should have been able to control their conduct and in some sense was responsible for it. Their question concerned why His disciples failed to observe the rules of conduct established by learned rabbis of the past, especially in regard to ceremonial cleansing of the hands before eating. This had nothing to do with sanitary considerations and was not in any way commanded in Levitical ordinances.

Though the scribes and Pharisees attacked on the level of failure to observe human regulations, Jesus counterattacked on the level of deliberate Pharisaical breaking of commandments detailed in the Word of God. In fact, it was not just a minor commandment but one of the Ten Commandments given at Sinai that they were accused of breaking (see Exod. 20:12; 21:17; Deut. 5:16).

Honoring one's father and mother involved helping to provide for their needs. The scribes and Pharisees had found a way around that responsibility by declaring that assets needed by their parents had been dedicated to God, and thus their parents could not lay claim to them. In this way they had shirked a divinely commanded obligation and thereby had set aside or invalidated the Word of God. Jesus went on to score their hypocrisy and cited Isaiah 29:13 as just as applicable to Messiah's contemporaries as it was to Isaiah's: they went through the motions of worship, but their hearts were not right before God; their traditions were man-made rules.

Having delivered a stinging denunciation of the Pharisees as "hypocrites," Jesus turned His attention to the crowd standing nearby and called them to center stage. Then He declared, "What goes into a man's mouth does not make him 'unclean,' but what comes out of his mouth, that is what makes him 'unclean'" (NIV). The Pharisees were still standing on the edge of the crowd and heard this pronouncement (v. 12). They were deeply offended by it because they believed that food touched by ceremonially unclean hands became unclean and defiled the person eating it. Jesus is saying in effect that defilement is spiritual, not physical. Food itself is amoral, intrinsically neither good nor bad. Jesus is not declaring that all Levitical distinctions have now come to an end. Rather, defilement comes not from Levitically unclean foods but from the rebelliousness of heart of the individual who flies in the face of God's specific commandment not to eat.

The spotlight shifts again, this time from the crowd to the disciples. Jesus and the disciples have gone into a house (Mark 7:17), and the conversation is private. First the disciples seem to be worried that Jesus has offended a group of influential Pharisees. For His part Jesus is not impressed. First He pronounces their ultimate judgment: "Every plant which My heavenly Father did not plant shall be rooted up" (NASB). The figure seems to be similar to that of the parable of the wheat and the darnel (Matt. 13:24-30). Those who are not true believers, not planted by the Father, ultimately will be uprooted in judgment. Next, He commands that those teachers of the law be abandoned. And last, He asserts that their proud claim to insight into truth is spiritual blindness (see John 9:40-41). As blind guides they lead their blind fellows astray and all fall into an open "pit," perhaps symbolizing the pit of hell.

Without debating Jesus' condemnation of the Pharisees, Peter asks for clarification of the parable spoken to the crowd. In a word, Jesus had sought to point out the mistake of teaching that ceremonial defilement brought moral and spiritual defilement. And He seems to be saying in His rebuke to Peter that spiritually perceptive persons should grasp that principle. Then He goes on to observe that "everything that goes into the mouth passes into the stomach and is eliminated" (NASB); it goes through the normal process of nature. In no way does it involve the heart; therefore it cannot defile (cf. Mark 7:18-19). But what comes "out of the mouth" proceeds from the "heart," the whole corrupt or depraved inner nature. From this source spring evil thoughts, which give rise to a variety of sinful words and deeds and which breach the sixth, seventh, eighth, and ninth commandments. The appearance of "murders," "adulteries," and other sins in the plural indicates the different instances and kinds of sins in such categories. In verse 20 Jesus brings the discussion to a close with an emphatic reassertion of His original declaration.

2. *Withdrawal to Phoenicia* (15:21-28). The confrontation with scribes and Pharisees from Jerusalem underscores the fact that opposition to Jesus was heightening. As opposition increased, so did the

realization that Jesus' time on earth was growing shorter. And the need for preparing the disciples to function on their own grew more crucial. To train the disciples further, Jesus took them northward into Lebanon where there was a greater chance that they would not be disturbed. As is clear from Mark 7:31, Jesus took the Twelve through southern Lebanon; subsequently they moved eastward around the foot of Mount Hermon and down the eastern shore of the Sea of Galilee.

Before the group actually got into Lebanon, a "Canaanite woman came out" to them. Evidently she was not only a Gentile but also a descendant of the earlier Canaanite stock of the area; thus she was not part of the Greek migration that had been moving into the area in recent centuries. Probably Mark's reference to her as Greek applies only to the fact that she was a Gentile. Although Jesus sought privacy, He could not be hid (Mark 7:24). Since many from the region of Tyre and Sidon already had benefited from His ministry (Mark 3:8), He was not completely unknown in this area. The woman's address as "Lord, Son of David" shows that she knew about the messianic hopes of Israel and accepted the belief that Jesus was indeed the Messiah. Her problem was that her daughter was demon-possessed.

At first Jesus did not answer. Then His disciples came to Him and "kept asking Him" to send her away. The request could be interpreted as a mere desire to get rid of the annoyance and a plea that He would ignore her. But it could just as well be viewed as a desire that He speedily conclude the matter and grant her request. This was quite a scene. Here were thirteen men walking along followed by a woman yelling "from behind them." If this kept up for long, it would not only embarrass them but also destroy any chance for privacy and training at His feet. To make it clear that Jesus' ministry was not now shifting to the Gentiles, He said, apparently to the disciples, "I was sent only to the lost sheep of the house of Israel."

By this time the woman had come up and prostrated herself at Jesus' feet, crying for help. Still primarily responding to the disciples, but speaking so she could hear, Jesus said that it was not "good to take the children's bread and throw it to the pet dogs." He, of course, was referring to the Jews as children and Gentiles as dogs; but He used a term describing pet dogs of the household, not uncouth wild beasts of the street. She responded with a willingness to accept the position of a dog, only asking for some crumbs to be tossed from the table in her direction. Jesus honored her humility and faith and granted immediate healing. The healing was by remote control (cf. John 4:46-53; Luke 7:6-10), but the woman had absolute faith in Jesus' pronouncement of healing and went home to find that it was so.

3. *Feeding the 4,000* (15:29-39). Taking a circuitous route from the vicinity of Tyre and Sidon, Jesus and His disciples moved south along the eastern shore of the Sea of Galilee and went up into the hills. In the process He had apparently avoided the territory of Herod Antipas and was now in the region ruled by Herod Philip. As Jesus ministered in the rural area, multitudes came for healing and they were not disappointed. Their response was to glorify "the God of Israel," an implication that the crowds were largely Gentile. Allusion to numerous miracles in passages like this reminds us of the fact that the thirty-five miracles especially described in the four Gospels are only selections from the large number that Jesus performed.

Evidently most of those who had been healed and those who brought them remained with Jesus because a large crowd had been near Him "for three days." It is unwarranted to say, as many critics do, that this is just another account of the feeding of the 5,000 reported earlier. It is noteworthy that both Matthew and Mark record both the feeding of the 5,000 and the 4,000, and both state numerous differences between the accounts. Differences are charted here to support the contention that two separate miracles are intended. Moreover, Matthew quotes Jesus Himself as observing that the two are separate miracles (16:9-10).

Feeding of 5,000	*Feeding of 4,000*
1. Feeding at evening of day of arrival	1. Feeding after three days
2. Disciples evidence concern about needs of multitudes	2. Jesus raises question about feeding crowds
3. Impossibility of providing a little food for each one present	3. Impossibility of filling such a multitude
4. Available food: 5 breads and 2 fish	4. Available food: 7 breads and a few fish
5. Reclined on the grass: spring	5. Reclined on the bare ground: summer
6. Leftovers: 12 small basketfuls	6. Leftovers: 7 large basketfuls

7. Number fed: 5,000 besides   7. Number fed: 4,000 besides
   women and children   women and children
8. Jesus sent disciples back   8. Jesus went across the Sea
   across the Sea of Galilee alone   with the disciples
9. Crossed over to Capernaum   9. Crossed over to Magadan
                                    (not Magdala as in KJV),
                                    location unknown

In feeding the 4,000, Jesus does not complain that the disciples lack faith or have learned nothing from a previous similar miracle. Their attitude simply seems to be that they recognize their inability to provide for so many and leave the matter entirely in Jesus' hands. He functions much the same on this occasion as during the previous miracle: offering prayer, multiplying the food, and giving to the disciples who serve. Specific details of the miracle appear in the chart above.

C. Third Withdrawal, Peter's Confession, and the Transfiguration (16:1–17:24)

1. *Pharisees and Sadducees confront Jesus* (16:1-4). Just as the Pharisees accosted Jesus prior to His second withdrawal, they also came to confront Him before His third withdrawal. This time they were joined by their traditional foes, the Sadducees. It is amazing how Jesus' foes often buried traditional animosities in order to make a stronger case against Him. The Pharisees were supernaturalists and the Sadducees antisupernaturalists. They all came requesting, as the Pharisees had in 12:38-40, that Jesus make some sort of spectacular display of power that undoubtedly would be of heavenly origin.

In reply, Jesus rebuked His adversaries for their inability to interpret the "signs of the times" when they were able to predict the weather. They were able to determine when the same sign (redness of the sky) meant good or stormy weather, but they could not interpret the spiritual signs of the times: the preaching of John the Baptist, the fulfillment of Old Testament prophecies, and the appearance and work of Jesus. This generation would be granted no sign but that of the prophet Jonah. Evidently Jesus had in mind His resurrection (Matt. 12:40), the greatest of all signs. And perhaps there was an ominous tone in His voice; the risen Christ would one day judge the wicked. At least in 12:41 He followed the sign of the Resurrection with a comment on the Judgment. Then the Master summarily dismissed the Pharisees and

Sadducees and initiated another withdrawal into territory largely Gentile, where He could spend some time with His disciples.

2. *Conversation about leaven* (16:5-12). As the disciples crossed the lake of Galilee, evidently toward Bethsaida at its northeast edge en route to Caesarea Philippi, they discovered they had forgotten to take along any food. A search turned up only one of those flat pieces of Palestinian bread shaped like a pancake (Mark 8:14). In the midst of their consternation, Jesus issued a warning against the leaven of the Pharisees and Sadducees. Evidently the disciples failed to get the point because they were so distraught over their own lack of food. For this reason Jesus rebuked them for their lack of faith in Him to provide. He had multiplied the bread and fish for the 5,000 and the 4,000, and He was fully able to meet the disciples' needs. Finally it dawned on them that leaven referred to the corrupting influence of the teaching of the Pharisees (hypocritical legalism) and Sadducees (rationalism or worldly materialism).

3. *Peter's confession* (16:13-20). At length Jesus and the Twelve came to the environs of Caesarea Philippi, about twenty-five miles north of the Sea of Galilee. His visit to the area was largely confined to the outlying villages (Mark 8:27), which would have been more largely Jewish. Herod Philip had made the city itself, his capital, an essentially Gentile city and had named it after Augustus Caesar and himself.

There Jesus the Master Teacher sought to lead His disciples into a deeper spiritual perception by means of the question-and-answer method. He set up the conversation with a heavily weighted question: "Who do people say the Son of Man is?" Evidently Jesus had coined this title for Himself. Derived from Daniel 7:13-14, it had a messianic significance. As "the Son of man," He was truly human but more than merely human; in fact, He was "the Word . . . made flesh" (John 1:14), the Son of God as well as the Son of man. This messianic title denationalized Him and made Him more than the King of Israel; He was the ruler and judge of all mankind (cf. Matt. 24:30; 26:64).

Jesus did not ask His question to elicit information but to get the disciples to state the various inadequate opinions of the people and to declare their own true conviction. John the Baptist risen from the dead was especially the opinion of Herod Antipas (see Matt. 14:1-2). John came to prepare for the coming of Messiah; Jesus came to offer Himself as the Messiah. Elijah, whose appearance was to precede the day of the

Lord (Mal. 4:5-6), again could only herald the coming of Christ. Moreover, Elijah had wavered in his service to God; Jesus was the Messiah who would set His face like a flint to do what the Father called on Him to do. Jeremiah could predict the new covenant (31:31-34), but Jesus instituted it.

Probably in a fairly lengthy discussion, either Jesus or the disciples demonstrated the inadequacy of these and other suggestions. Finally Jesus asked them about their own belief as to His identity. Peter answered unequivocally, "You are the Christ, the Son of the living God." Doubtless the others concurred; at least there is no record to the contrary. What might have been going through the mind of Judas is an interesting subject of speculation. Peter declared that Jesus was the Christ, the Messiah, the Anointed One; but He was not merely a political Messiah, He was "the Son," the unique Son, "of God."

Jesus' response was first to accept Peter's confession. "Simon son of John" refers to Peter's natural state. In his unaided humanity ("flesh and blood") he did not arrive at this conclusion, but it came by divine revelation or illumination from "my Father in heaven."

Then Jesus proceeded to call attention to his name "Peter" (Greek, *Petros*) and said that on this "rock" (Greek, *petra)* "I will build my church." The Roman Catholic interpretation of this statement is that the rock is Peter who became bishop of Rome, that Christ was assigning him primacy in the church, that this primacy was transmissible to his successors, and that this primacy has been transmitted to the present pope. Protestants commonly have reacted so strongly against such a view that they have tried to eliminate Peter from the interpretation.

Some argue that the rock is Jesus Christ; but the passage views Christ as the architect who is doing the building, and He does not say, "I will build the church on Myself, the Rock." Though numerous passages refer to Him as the Chief Cornerstone (e.g., Matt. 21:42; Acts 4:11; Eph. 2:20; 1 Peter 2:4-7), and one reference alludes to Him as a foundation (1 Cor. 3:11), it does not seem adequate to designate Christ alone as the "rock."

Others have taught that the rock on which the church would be built was Peter's confession; and they have produced such passages as Acts 8:36-37; Romans 10:9-10; and 1 John 4:15 to support their position. This was the view of Martin Luther and a majority of the church fathers, including St. Augustine, Jerome, and Gregory the Great (Kuen, p. 112). Neither does this view seem to provide a completely

satisfactory solution. "Both the play upon the words and the natural reading of the passage are against it" (Vincent, p. 92).

Jesus addressed Peter, and Peter must somehow be included in any
proper interpretation of this passage. Jesus did not say, however, "You
are Peter and on you the church will be built"; so more than Peter must
be involved. *Petros* (Peter) is not a pebble but a piece of stone which, as
the classics show, a Greek warrior sometimes obtained by sticking the
tip of his sword into a ledge of rock (a *petra*) and twisting it. Of course
jagged pieces of rock were dislodged in other ways. Thus the *petros* is
part of the *petra*. Ephesians 2:20 says that the church is built on a
foundation of apostles and prophets. Put another way, one might say the
foundation course of masonry in the church consists of apostles and
prophets *(petra)*, of which Peter is one stone *(petros)*. On this occasion
as Jesus addressed Peter *(petros)*, He may have gestured toward the
whole group of apostles and said, "On this *petra* I will build my church."
The church itself would consist of living stones built up in a spiritual
building (1 Peter 2:4-5).

Actually, all these views may be brought together in a single
interpretation. On a rock base, Christ (Matt. 7:24-27; 1 Cor. 3:11),
a row of stones *(petra)* was laid as a first course of masonry. One of
these stones was Simon Peter *(petros)*; and it was on the basis of his
confession that he became a part of the church. In subsequent centuries living stones, as they make their confession, are placed into
upper courses of masonry as the walls of the church rise. Jesus
Christ as the Chief Cornerstone gives significance and symmetry to
the building.

The church is viewed as a new entity, yet future: "I will build."
Evidently the church began on the day of Pentecost. This may be
concluded from the fact that one gets into the church (the body of Christ)
by means of the baptism in or with the Holy Spirit (1 Cor. 12:13), that the
baptism of the Spirit is future in the Gospels (Matt. 3:11; Mark 1:8; Luke
3:16; John 1:33) and in Acts 1:5, and that it is past in Acts 11:15-16.
Pentecost seems to be the only logical place to begin the baptism of the
Holy Spirit. In passing, it should be noted that baptism must not be
confused with the filling of the Spirit or with some special spiritual
experience subsequent to conversion. Baptism of the Spirit in Scripture
refers to the act by which one is placed in the body of Christ, which is the
church.

"The gates of Hades will not overcome it" (NIV) or "The powers of the underworld shall never overthrow it" (Williams). The "gates of Hades" refers to the "throne, power, and dignity of the infernal kingdom" (Vincent, p. 96). The kingdom of Hades assaults the church; and while it may win some temporary successes, we have Christ's promise that it will never destroy the church.

"I will give you the keys of the kingdom of heaven." To a Jew of that day this statement had a specific meaning. Carr observes: "A key was given to a Scribe when admitted to his office as a symbol of his authority to open the treasury of divine oracles . . . the key was symbolic of office and authority generally" (p. 212). See Isaiah 22:22 and Revelation 3:7.

At some time in the near future, Peter, as steward of the kingdom of heaven, would have the privilege of inserting a key in the lock and opening the door of the kingdom of heaven as he preached Christ crucified, buried, and risen for the remission of sins. This is usually interpreted as occurring on the day of Pentecost when he opened the door wide to the Jews in Jerusalem (Acts 2), and in Caesarea when he opened the door to the Gentiles (Acts 10:1–11:18; 14:27; 15:7,14).

The power of binding and loosing is here given to Peter and later to all the disciples (Matt. 18:18); so whatever it involved, it did not make Peter the ruler of the church in some final sense. "'To bind' (cp. ch. xxiii.4) is to impose an obligation as binding; 'to loose' is to declare a precept not binding" (Carr, p. 212). "No other terms were in more constant use in Rabbinic canon-law than those of *binding* and *loosing*. They represented the *legislative* and *judicial* powers of the Rabbinic office" (Vincent, p. 96).

"Whatsoever" is in the neuter and refers to things, not to persons; it refers to an administrative authority in the church. The force of the original is correctly brought out in the NASB: "Whatsoever you shall bind on earth shall have been bound in heaven; and whatsoever you shall loose on earth shall have been loosed in heaven." The decisions the apostles rendered would agree with what God Himself had already determined; this would be possible as the disciples were led by the Holy Spirit in their exercise of authority in the church. Probably a good example of this binding and loosing action is the decision at the Council of Jerusalem in Acts 15.

Jesus concluded this dialogue "by giving the disciples strict orders" to refrain from telling anyone that He was the Messiah. They were not to excite the multitudes with the kind of announcement that would stir their political sensitivities. They could not yet understand that the Messiah's first task was to redeem the souls of sinful humanity. In a few months, after He had paid the penalty for sin and had gone home to heaven, it would be quite in order to spread abroad the confession that Jesus was "the Christ."

4. *Jesus' prediction of His death and resurrection* (16:21-23). In Jesus' instruction of the disciples, it was logical to follow recognition of Him as Messiah with a prediction of His suffering and death because as Messiah He was especially commissioned to be the Savior. Although He "began" at this point to teach them openly of His passion, hints of His death had come earlier (John 2:19; 3:12-16; Matt. 9:15; John 6:45-51). His suffering would occur at the hands of the "elders" (lay leaders), "chief priests" (Sadducees), and "scribes" (Pharisees)—the three groups in the Sanhedrin, the chief council of the Jews. The place of His suffering would be Jerusalem and the extent would be unto death—but not for long. He would rise "on the third day."

The concept of the Messiah as a suffering Savior rather than a political deliverer was foreign, not only to the multitudes, but even to the disciples. Peter took Jesus aside to remonstrate with Him: "This shall never happen to you!" (NIV). Though he spoke in private, Peter may well have had the support of the others on this occasion. Certainly they had no more spiritual perception than he. At any rate, it is clear that Jesus rebuked Peter within clear view of the rest (Mark 8:33), but it is not clear whether they were within earshot. "Get out of my way, Satan!" Peter had become an instrument of Satan, trying to dissuade Jesus from becoming the Redeemer. Satan also had wanted Him to accept the kingdom without the cross (Matt. 4:8-10). "You do not have in mind the things of God, but the things of man" (NIV). You do not understand God's plan for solving the sin problem through the death of Christ; but as men do, you view the Messiah as a person of great power who could set up His rule on earth without suffering. It is sobering to see that one who was capable of receiving divine illumination (v. 17) and of being an instrument in the hand of God could so readily become an instrument of Satan.

5. *The imperative of discipleship* (16:24-28). As is clear from Mark 8:34, at this point Jesus and the disciples were joined by a crowd of others. Then Jesus issued His famous call to discipleship. A true disciple must "deny himself," must renounce any claim to himself, and must recognize instead the lordship of Christ over him. This does not mean a self-abnegation that destroys one's God-given personality and distinc-

tive gifts, but it involves making oneself completely available to the Master. Cross bearing applies to the trials which come to the believer because of his Christian profession and which can be escaped by denying the obligation of discipleship. "Whoever wants to save his [physical] life" and ignores the claims of Christ may do so, but he will miss the life that is eternal or miss the fuller life. "Whoever is willing to lose his life," either in the sacrifice of personal ambition or wealth or martyrdom, for the sake of Christ or the promulgation of His message (the gospel), will find it, safe and blessed with God.

"What benefit would accrue to a man, if he gains the whole world and forfeits his higher life?" If one's desire for the plaudits of the world and its material benefits leads him away from the life of discipleship, he will then forfeit his soul or his higher life. As Kent observes, "The figure pictures a business transaction in which a man exchanges his very life (including the soul) for this world's attractions. What would such a man use to buy back his *psychē* [soul]?" (p. 960). True disciples who may sacrifice much for the Lord have the promise of full reward at His coming (v. 27).

The prediction that some present would not die before they saw Him coming in His kingdom is most naturally interpreted to refer to the three members of the inner circle. Shortly they were to witness the glorified Christ at the Transfiguration, which was a foretaste of the coming of Christ in His kingdom.

6. *The Transfiguration* (17:1-13). "After six days" serves as a link between announcement of the Passion and the vision of glory, between Peter's and the Father's declaration of Jesus' divine sonship, and between the disciples' recognition by faith of Jesus' messiahship and their apprehension by sight of who He really was. "Six days" does not conflict with the "about eight days" of Luke 9:28 because Jewish reckoning counted a part of a day as a day; Luke apparently included the parts of days on either end of the week.

Jesus chose the inner circle of Peter, James, and John to be special witnesses of His glorification; these He also chose to be with Him for the raising of Jairus' daughter and the agony in the Garden of Gethsemane. The "high mountain" can hardly be Mount Tabor in Galilee, traditional site of the Transfiguration. This seems so because He was in a period of withdrawal from Galilee and because at this time a fortress occupied the summit of Tabor. Possibly Jesus led the disciples up one of the spurs of Mount Hermon, but one of the ridges immediately adjacent to Caesarea

Philippi would fill all the requirements of the narrative.

While Jesus was praying (Luke 9:29), He was "transformed." The word translated "transformed" *(metamorpheō)* indicates an actual change of form, not a mere change of appearance or a masking of His ordinary appearance. Probably Jesus prayed for a long time and the disciples dozed off (Luke 9:32). Suddenly they were startled to full alertness at the sight of Jesus. His face was as brilliant as the sun, and His clothes "had the translucent whiteness of pure light" (Lenski, p. 652). Verse 2 seems to indicate that it was now night; and after this nighttime revelation, "the next day" (Luke 9:37) they all came down from the mountain. Even more astounding, Moses and Elijah, representatives of the Law and Prophets, stood conversing with Jesus. How the disciples knew who these august personages were is not stated. Luke reveals the subject of this history-making conversation: His impending death at Jerusalem (Luke 9:31).

Peter seems to have felt that he had to say something. He "answered," responded or reacted to the scene; he had not been addressed. Awed by the glory of the moment, Peter sought to prolong it; and thus he made the suggestion that he be allowed to make booths for all three of them. The word for *booth* indicates a hut of boughs of the sort constructed for the Feast of Tabernacles. Peter said nothing about booths for the disciples; presumably they would sleep on the ground.

While Jesus was still speaking, a bright cloud enveloped the group, signifying the presence of the Father. And from the cloud came the divine pronouncement as at the baptism (Matt. 3:17): "This is My beloved Son in whom I am well pleased. Keep on listening to Him." The command is durative and applies even to the present time. The Father once more fully placed His seal of approval on the Son—for the benefit of the Son who was about to undergo intense suffering and for the disciples who would share the trauma of that moment and who soon would lose the blessing of His physical presence.

The disciples, unable to stand before such august majesty (cf. Isa. 6), fell down on their faces in fear. Then Jesus came over and touched them. On His order they rose and cast away their fears. Then He was alone once more and resumed His normal appearance.

The next morning as they came down the mountainside, Jesus strictly ordered the disciples not to tell anyone what they had seen until "the Son of man has been raised from the dead." The reason is not hard to discover. The rest of the disciples, and even more so the multitudes,

would have had their messianic expectations whipped up to uncontrol-
lable proportions; all that frenzy would have gotten in the way of His
work of atonement. It is not clear whether the trio understood what the
rising from the dead meant, but at least they evidently kept the secret
well until Jesus wanted it revealed (see 2 Peter 1:16-18; John 1:14).

As the trio came down the mountain, they were puzzled. They had
just seen Elijah but were committed to silence about the fact. Yet the
scribes, following Malachi 4:5, taught that Elijah must come before
Messiah would be revealed. If Elijah had come, the disciples should
shout it from the housetops in order that Messiah be recognized and
received. Jesus answered to the effect that Elijah would indeed come in
the last day, but in a sense "Elijah has already come." John the Baptist
had come in the spirit and power of Elijah (Luke 1:17) and did "restore
all things," brought about a spiritual restoration and turned the hearts of
the people to God. But "they," the scribes, Pharisees, Sadducees,
Herod, and the people generally, "did not recognize him" and killed
him. In like manner the Son of man was destined to be executed. The
disciples understood the identification of Elijah with John, but probably
their perception stopped there—not quite extending to the imminent
death of the Messiah.

7. *Healing of the epileptic* (17:14-21). Mountaintop experiences
help to prepare for the valleys. And while some believers may be
enjoying mountaintop experiences, others are in the valley facing suffering and failure on the front line of service. Raphael's *Transfiguration*
portrays the fact well by including both the tranquil scene on the
mountain and the scene of defeat and frustration below.

To get the full story of this event, it is necessary to compare these
verses with Mark 9:14-29 and Luke 9:37-42. Jesus and His three com-
panions came upon the other nine disciples engaged in a discussion with
some scribes in the presence of a crowd of people. The topic of the
dispute was why the nine did not have power to deliver a demon-
possessed boy. A demon had rendered the boy deaf and dumb, and
periodically it threw him into convulsions resembling epileptic fits or
worse.

Evidently the disciples had acted on Jesus' command given in
Matthew 10:8 to "drive out demons," but they had been unsuccessful.
Jesus rebuked the nine as "faithless" and "perverse" and commanded
that the boy be brought to Him. The command is in itself a promise of

response to the agonized plea of the father. Then Jesus completely healed the boy.

Later the disciples privately asked Jesus, "Why couldn't we drive it out?" (NIV). Perhaps the answer is implicit in the question. The stress seemed to be on their own efforts. "We" may not be successful in our work for God because we do it in our own strength instead of drawing heavily on divine resources. Jesus answered them bluntly: "Because you have so little faith." Clearly this was not a lack of saving faith but a lack of faith in the power of God to work miracles. The fault lay not in the power of God but in their faith, which even if minute (size of a mustard seed) could remove mountains, i.e., make great difficulties vanish. "Nothing shall be impossible for you" is not a promise to Jesus' followers that they could do all sorts of silly things such as moving mountains around but that by faith they would be able to do effectively—sometimes even charismatically—what God called them to do in the course of their service for Him. Verse 21 apparently was not a part of Matthew's original manuscript; scholars generally conclude that it was interpolated from Mark 9:29. Thus, though it does not belong to the text here, it was part of the story of the epileptic.

8. *Second Passion announcement* (17:22-23). A lapse of time occurred between verses 21 and 22. The apostolic company had traveled southwestward toward Capernaum. As they "wandered about in Galilee," Jesus made His second Passion announcement (cf. 16:21). This time He said He was "about to be delivered" (the time was short and a betrayer was implied) "into the hands of men" (the Sanhedrin). His death and resurrection on the third day was repeated. In answering the call to discipleship, the Twelve had given up all to follow Him; their security was now in Him. For Him to die was to bring the collapse of their little world. Moreover, their view of the Messiah, as was true of Jews generally at that time, was not that of a suffering servant but a reigning king. His death at the height of His power and popularity did not fit their conception of the Messiah and was incredible to them. His resurrection was even more incredible. So they "were filled with grief."

D. Return to Capernaum and Instruction of the Disciples (17:24–18:35)

Having completed His third withdrawal with His disciples, Jesus returned to Capernaum briefly before starting for Jerusalem and His Passion. But even though He was "at home" for a while, Jesus did not give Himself to the multitudes as He had before; His concentration on training of the Twelve continued paramount.

1. *The temple tax* (17:24-27). The tax question raised here had nothing to do with loyalty to local government or to Rome; it involved Jesus' support of the temple in Jerusalem. On the basis of Exodus 30:13-14, every adult male Jew was expected to give annually a half shekel (or Greek two-drachma piece) to the temple treasury. The collectors of such taxes asked Peter somewhere on the street whether Jesus was accustomed to paying this tax. Peter answered, "Yes." The motive for the question is not clear. The collectors did not seem to have been trying to trap Jesus. Perhaps they only wondered whether He followed the teachings of the establishment on this point.

When Peter entered the house, Jesus read his thoughts and spoke first, showing by illustration that the sons of kings do not need to pay "duty and taxes." By implication Jesus was saying that He as the Son of God did not need to pay taxes for the support of His Father's house. But lest He "offend" or seem to be guilty of disrespect for God's house, He arranged payment.

The whole situation surrounding payment demonstrates Jesus' deity, however, and thus His right to exemption from the tax. First, He showed omniscience by reading Peter's thoughts. Second, He likewise demonstrated omniscience in knowing which fish had the coin in its mouth. Third, He evidenced omnipotence in bringing about the logistics of the miracle: the fish with a coin at the place and time that Peter would come by to make the catch. The coin would be a shekel, or four-drachma piece, that would provide payment for both Jesus and Peter. If Peter had been worried about where either he or Jesus would get the money to pay the temple tax for that year, his worries were over.

2. *Greatest in the kingdom* (18:1-20). As is clear from Mark 9:33-34, the background for the question posed in Matthew 18:1 was a debate among the disciples as to which of them would be greatest in the kingdom. The question was particularly ill-timed because it came right after Jesus' second announcement of His coming sacrifice for all mankind. Jesus' answer came in the form of another object lesson. He called a little child to stand among them while He spoke to them. The house in Capernaum where the event occurred may have been Peter's, and the child may have been Peter's son. Jesus asserted: "Unless you are converted and become as little children, you will not enter the kingdom of heaven," much less be great in the kingdom (the messianic kingdom

they expected to be set up). The new birth (John 3:3) must be accompanied by a childlikeness.

The disciples, like little children, were to be characterized by simple trust in the Father and complete dependence upon Him for everything. Like a little child, a disciple had nothing to offer the Father but love and trust. The disciple is able to do nothing, to earn nothing, and must receive all spiritual benefits as a gift. Therefore he has nothing of which to boast and should be characterized by humility.

In verse 5 Jesus turned to a discussion of believers or disciples who were characterized by the childlike qualities He had been insisting on. "Whoever welcomes" or receives or grants kindness to such a believer "in my name," because he belongs to Christ, is regarded as having shown kindness to Christ Himself. Not only should one show kindness to another believer, but he should also avoid causing him to stumble, making his discipleship more difficult, or treating him harshly and contemptuously so as to tempt him to turn from his faith. Bruce solemnly warns, "The pride and selfish ambition of those who pass for eminent Christians make many infidels" (p. 237).

Let one who puts a stone of stumbling in the path of another have a large millstone hung about his neck and dumped in the sea. This was not a small grinding stone driven by hand but a large one requiring a donkey to turn. Such a large stone would guarantee that a person tied to it would not again rise to the surface. It is inevitable that "stumbling-blocks"— snares and temptations—shall come; but woe to the one who is a *willing* medium of such entrapments—either a person of "the world," an unbeliever, or a believer. The offender is responsible for his guilt. One should take drastic steps to avoid being a stumbling block to another (vv. 8-9). See comments on Matthew 5:29-30, where similar phraseology is used.

One should be careful not to despise or show contempt for other believers, however spiritually immature or difficult they may be, for they are special objects of God's love. In fact, God has delegated angels to care for believers (see Heb. 1:14). Apparently, however, angels are to watch over believers as a group; there is no evidence that each believer has a guardian angel. (Verse 11 does not appear in the best manuscripts of Matthew and seems to have been an interpolation from Luke 19:10.)

Not only does God care for the most lowly believer who seeks to know and serve Him, but He is also concerned for wayward and erring ones. The parable of the straying sheep beautifully illustrates this truth. No effort should be spared to rescue such straying ones. While in Luke 15:4-7 this parable is used to illustrate the salvation of sinners, here it portrays concern over reclaiming the wayward.

There is a progression of thought here. Disciples who wish to be great are told that first they must accept and show kindness to other believers (vv. 5-9), facilitating their Christian walk and doing everything possible to avoid being a stumbling block to them. Second, they are not to despise or show contempt for other believers but are to offer help to those who may be in danger of going astray or who may have gone astray (vv. 10-14). Third, they are taught what to do if one Christian sins against another (vv. 15-17).

Evidently the sin in view in verses 15-17 is not a careless slight or an affront to an oversensitive believer. It is a sin of some seriousness that would be clearly recognizable as such by numbers of individuals if they knew about it. One who is wronged first should go to his brother and "show him his fault" with a view to bringing conviction. He should observe strict privacy in order to shield his brother and make it easier for him to confess the sin. If after some effort the erring brother remains adamant, the wronged one is then to take along two or three others as witnesses (Deut. 19:15). These individuals can fill an important role if the case is ever inquired into again. Their testimony will be especially important if the case does come up before the whole church.

If, as a course of last resort, the sinner refuses to listen to the whole church, he is to be treated as a "Gentile or a tax-collector," as one who had separated himself from the fellowship of believers. Gentiles were outside the covenant blessings of Israel, and publicans likewise were cut off from acceptance by the Jewish community (Matt. 9:10). Of course many sins are not very private or against only one person, but principles enumerated here may be applied to a wide variety of situations.

When carefully related to the foregoing verses dealing with discipline in the church, the interpretation of verse 18 becomes fundamentally simple. The binding and loosing evidently has to do with judicial actions of the church as a whole and is not a function of apostles only or church leaders only. Moreover, the church does not have the power to make up principles as it goes along; binding and loosing in the Greek are in the future perfect tense. The NASB has the correct translation: "Whatever you shall bind on earth shall have been bound in heaven; and whatever you loose on earth shall have been loosed in heaven."

As noted above, sins to be judged must clearly be sins by divine definition; the sinfulness of an act and its consequences have been established by God "in heaven." Neither the church nor its hierarchy has the right to decide what is or is not sin; actions taken on earth are to be in full accord with positions already established in heaven. Furthermore, the verse says "whatever," not "whoever you shall bind." As Lenski observes, "The church judges, not the hearts, but the words and deeds" (p. 704). The power of binding and loosing first given to Peter in Matthew 16:19 was not to be exercised by him alone, the Twelve alone, or leaders of the church in apostolic succession alone, but by the entire church.

The promise that prayer will be answered if "two agree" (vv. 19-20) has to do especially with disciplinary cases and "provides additional proof that the prayerful decisions of the congregation in disciplinary actions will be divinely honored" (Kent, p. 962). But of course the passage applies to more than disciplinary matters. And it must be placed alongside other clear teachings on prayer, e.g., that it be offered according to His will (1 John 5:14).

"I am with them" (v. 20) refers to Christ's promise to be present in power in some special sense when concerted prayer takes place. It is not necessary for the believer to pray that Christ be present in his life because Christ indwells every believer (e.g., Gal. 2:20; Col. 1:27), and He has promised never to leave or forsake us (Matt. 28:20; Heb. 13:5).

3. *Forgiveness* (18:21-35). After some break in Jesus' discussion with the disciples, Peter raised a question. Apparently thinking about the person who had been wronged by his brother (v. 15), he asked how many times one should forgive those who have sinned against another. "Seven times" is a generous upping of the traditional Jewish allowance of three times. The answer of "seventy times seven" probably is meant to cover forgiveness of all wrongs because no one would keep a careful tally of such large numbers of offenses.

Then to illustrate the point Jesus told a parable about an unmerciful servant. In it a creditor, a king (God Himself), remitted or forgave a very large debt owed him. But the forgiven servant as a creditor himself failed to remit a lesser debt owed him and threw his debtor into prison. When the first creditor heard about it, he retaliated in like fashion. Jesus dealt here with the hatefulness of an unforgiving spirit and conveyed the idea that if God forgave us so much, we should be willing to forgive all who sin against us. Our sin debt to God was so horrendous and so totally beyond our ability to pay or to atone for that the sins which others commit against us pale by comparison.

The point of the parable seems to be abundantly clear down to verses 34-35. Verse 34 says that the one with an unforgiving spirit will be turned "over to the torturers until he should repay" all he owes. Some have found support here for the doctrine of purgatory, but that is impossible. One can never pay God what he owes. The individual is spiritually bankrupt and has literally nothing to pay. Moreover, there is no hint that the sufferings alluded to will occur after death. Therefore it seems equally unlikely that the passage refers to eternal punishment.

The person in question evidently is a believer: he has had a large debt remitted; he has received mercy. Punishment is for an unforgiving spirit and the intimation is that he may still repent of that sin. Evidently the torments are "temporal evils visited upon unforgiving believers by their 'heavenly Father'" (Kent, p. 962). Sometimes God has to bring judgment upon us for our waywardness (1 Cor. 11:30-32), sin which does not bring loss of salvation but loss of fellowship with God and with men. Such an interpretation fits well in this context where relations between believers have been discussed (cf. vv. 15-20).

For Further Study

1. Compare Jesus' two rejections at Nazareth.

2. Make a study of the geography of the Sea of Galilee and meteorological conditions of the area.

3. Make a study of the miracles discussed in this chapter. Observe such things as Jesus' method, the disciples' response, reaction of those benefited, and other topics of your own choosing.

4. What opposition to Jesus appears in this chapter and how does He handle it?

5. Describe the experiences Peter had in this chapter.

PART THREE: *Messiah's Ministry in Jerusalem*

Chapter 10

Messiah's Journey to Jerusalem
(Matthew 19:1–20:34)

A. Lessons of Life (19:1-26)

1. *Traveling and healing* (19:1-2). With Matthew 19:1, Jesus completed His ministry in Galilee and started on the road to Jerusalem and the Crucifixion. Most of the versions of this verse need to be corrected because they imply that Judea extended east of the Jordan, which it never did; and certainly Matthew knew that it did not. The proper translation should read, "Went to the boundaries of Judea, beyond the Jordan." "Beyond the Jordan" modifies "went" and indicates that Jesus took the route to Judea which lay east of the Jordan instead of the one that passed through Samaria. This road through Perea brought Jesus into territory where He had not previously ministered.

As in Galilee, crowds followed Jesus and He healed their sick. Though His journey through this region was somewhat extended, Matthew concentrates on the training of the Twelve. Some of the events he omits include two brief visits to Jerusalem (John 7:8-10; 10:22-39), the raising of Lazarus (John 11:1-46), and the retirement to Ephraim (John 11:54).

2. *The divorce question* (19:3-12). As Jesus moved slowly through Perea, some Pharisees came "to test" Him. Of the same stripe as those in Galilee and Judea, these Pharisees sought to ask Him a question they thought He could not answer without great harm to Himself: "Is it right for a man to divorce his wife for any cause?" Would Jesus come down on the side of the school of Hillel which permitted divorce for almost any reason, or would He concur with the school of Shammai which allowed divorce for adultery only. Either answer would involve Him in Jewish party disputes. Prohibition of all divorce would put Him in contradic-

tion of the law of Moses (Deut. 24:1). And any pronouncement on divorce was risky in the territory of Herod Antipas, whose marriage to Herodias had brought the condemnation of John the Baptist and his martyrdom.

Jesus appealed to a higher and absolute law which antidated that of Moses. Harking back to Genesis 1:27 and 2:24, He stated that God created male and female for each other. They were to cut family ties and to become one flesh—in a sexual union that constitutes them as "no longer two but one." This arrangement, this union, is of God's doing; and the one who separates what God put together is flying in the face of God Himself.

Then the Pharisees asked, in effect, why Moses commanded divorce. Of course they did not get the point; Moses was not trying to authorize divorce but to protect wives from the caprice of their husbands and provide them with a legal document that would indicate their status. Jesus corrected the Pharisees by observing that Moses did not "command" but "permitted" divorce "because of your moral perversity" (Williams), a condition which occurred because of the fall of man. Jesus continued, "Whoever divorces his wife, except for immorality, and marries another commits adultery" (NASB). So the only basis for divorce is immorality or unfaithfulness of the marriage partner; and one divorcing his wife for any other reason commits a terrible wrong against her and against her second husband if she marries again. All are counted guilty of adultery.

The disciples reacted to this very restrictive pronouncement by concluding that it was then better not to marry at all. They were so imbued with Jewish laxness that they felt it was better not to marry than to be saddled with a wife they might like to get rid of. Jesus responded, "It is not every man who has the capacity to carry out this saying." "This saying" is commonly referred to the apostles' idea that the single state may be preferred. Jesus went on to observe that some may not marry because they have congenital defects or because they have been castrated; and a few may refrain from marriage in order to devote themselves more effectively to the service of God (e.g., 1 Cor. 7:7-35). But most will marry, and what He said about marriage and divorce applied to them.

3. *Blessing of children* (19:13-15). The narrative passes from teaching on the divine ordering of marriage to the love of little children. Though this event appears to have taken place out-of-doors, the parallel

account in Mark 10:10 shows that it actually took place in a house. Thus it was possible for the disciples to turn away some of those who came. Why they sought to hinder the blessing of the little ones is not clear. Perhaps they wanted to spare the Master this added burden and intrusion on His privacy. Possibly they wanted more of His time for instruction. If the children were mostly babes in arms who presumably could not benefit much from His ministry to them, they may have thought He should have been freed for attention to older persons.

Jesus rebuked the disciples and welcomed the little ones, "for of such is the kingdom of heaven." They serve as examples of believers. He did not say "of these" but "of such." That is to say, the kingdom of heaven is composed not of children as children but of individuals with such characteristics: humility, trust, and a willingness to accept the gift of God's grace.

4. *The rich young man* (19:16-26). Having left the house and the place where He was, Jesus encountered a rich young man. From Luke we learn that this man was a ruler (18:18)—of what is not clear. Commonly it is assumed that he was a ruler of a synagogue, but if so he should have been older. Approaching Jesus on the basis of works righteousness, he asked, "What good thing shall I do, that I may have eternal life?" He did not seem to have any doubt in his mind about how to obtain salvation. Jesus said in effect, "Why do you ask Me about what is good? God is the only good Being, and His word tells us the good He would have us do: keep the commandments."

Steeped in the multiplicity of Pharisaic regulations, the young man asked, "Which ones?" Jesus then alluded to the sixth, seventh, eighth, ninth, and fifth commandments and a summary of the second table of the law: "Love your neighbor as yourself." Jesus was not really indicating that salvation was by works, but for the moment He accepted the questioner on his own grounds in order to show him the true nature of his need.

The young man responded, "All these have I kept"; as far as he knew, he had conformed to the externals of the law. But he sensed that such conformity was not enough and that is why he had come to Jesus in the first place; so he asked, "What do I still lack?" Now came the real test: If you want to be complete or without lack, "go," "sell," "give"—divest yourself of your wealth. This the rich young man was unwilling to do.

The point here is not that giving away his wealth would bring the man salvation, but wealth had become his god. Thus he had broken the first table of the law: "You shall have no other gods before me" (Exod. 20:3). Salvation would come as the young man obeyed the second of Jesus' exhortations: "Come, follow me"—put your complete trust in Me. God does not ask those who come to Him today to take a vow of poverty. He demands only that they give Him first place in their lives and put at His disposal their worldly goods—and themselves. Christians cannot serve God and riches (Matt. 6:24).

As the young man went his way without attaining his goal, Jesus had some comments on the difficulty of the rich entering the kingdom of heaven. The danger for the rich lies in the temptation to trust in material resources rather than in God. In fact, "it is easier for a camel to go through a needle's eye"; it is easier for the largest animal in Palestine to go through the eye of a sewing needle than for a rich man trusting in his riches to enter the kingdom of heaven.

This statement thoroughly startled the disciples because the prevailing view was that the wealthy had something to commend them before God and their wealth was some evidence of God's favor upon them. In response to the disciples' question, "Who then can be saved" if the wealthy cannot, Jesus answered, in effect, "Man may not have the power to get himself saved, but God has the power to effect deliverance, to bestow salvation."

B. Promises and Parables (19:27–20:19)

1. *Followers of Christ* (19:27-30). Suddenly it occurred to Peter that He and the other eleven had met the requirements of discipleship enunciated to the rich young ruler. In a complete break with the past they "left all and followed Him." Peter then asked what would be their reward for service. Jesus did not rebuke him for inferior motives but promised reward for discipleship. First, there was a prediction to be fulfilled in the indefinite future. In the "regeneration" (cf. Acts 3:21) or "in the new order of life" (Williams), evidently the millennium, when all things will be brought in subservience to Christ, the disciples will have a preferred position, "sitting on twelve thrones, judging the twelve tribes of Israel." Second, all who have given up homes, relatives, or property for Jesus' sake will receive the optimum level of return ("a hundredfold"), either in the present age (Mark 10:30) or in the life to come. For instance, in return for homes and families given up come new spiritual relationships of brothers and sisters and mothers and fathers in

Christ. And often kinfolk forsaken for Christ are later won for Christ. Third, there is the promise of eternal life.

Verse 30 is susceptible to numerous interpretations. Williams translates it thus: "But many who are first now will be last then, and many who are last now will be first then." The implied meaning is that many like the rich young ruler and others of stature in this world will have no rank in the coming kingdom (will not be in it); others like the apostles will have special positions. In a different vein Kent observes, "Here the context suggests its application to those who had first (in time) established their relation to Christ and might develop an attitude of presumption" (p. 964). Bruce concludes, "The connection of thought is: self-sacrifice such as yours, Peter, has a great reward, but beware of self-complacency, which may so vitiate the quality of service as to make one first in sacrifice last in the esteem of God" (p. 253). The verse is repeated again in Matthew 20:16 and the intervening parable illustrates the point.

2. *Laborers in the vineyard* (20:1-16). Apparently during the period of grape harvest, when an abundance of extra labor was required, a vineyard owner kept going out and hiring additional workers during the course of the day. Early in the morning he hired workers who insisted on a definite wage and agreed on a denarius for the day (cf. Matt. 19:27—"What, then, shall be ours?"). Those hired at the sixth, ninth, and eleventh hours did not bargain for a definite wage. At the end of the day the vineyard owner paid the workers, beginning with those hired at the eleventh hour and ultimately giving all the same wage.

When murmuring arose over this seeming unfairness, the owner reminded those who served longest that he had a right to do as he wished about remuneration as long as he kept his bargain with the workers. The message of the parable is this: While God keeps His promises to those who serve Him, He alone can judge what is just. Moreover, God is sovereign and will retain His rights in the matter of rewards. He will reward the work done, but He will reward according to His sovereign will.

No one has a right to demand rewards for service to God. Since Christ declared, "Without me ye can do nothing" (John 15:5), all our successes are achieved by His strength. Thus, any reward must be bestowed solely on the basis of God's grace—not because of our merit. Moreover, "work done in a legal spirit does not count in the Kingdom of God. In reward it is last, or even nowhere. This is the *trend* of the parable, and so viewed it has a manifest connection with Peter's self-complacent question" (Bruce, p. 256). A believer has no right to complain about the grace of God bestowed on another believer.

That the denarius given the worker is salvation cannot be substantiated because the parable then would be made to teach that individuals must work for their salvation. Neither can the parable be made to teach that there is no difference in rewards for believers. Jesus had just promised the disciples a special position in the coming kingdom. And the two major statements on the judgment of believers' works indicate a difference of rewards (1 Cor. 3:11-15; 2 Cor. 5:10). But some blessings in the kingdom will be enjoyed equally by all believers regardless of how early or late in life they may have put their faith in Chirst and entered the Master's service.

3. *Third Passion announcement* (20:17-19). The first Passion announcement (16:21) had been very general: Jesus would suffer many things at the hands of the Sanhedrin, be killed, and be resurrected on the third day. The second (17:22-23) added the detail of His betrayal into the hands of men. Now as Jesus and the Twelve were "going up to Jerusalem" among the throngs of pilgrims who were coming for Passover, Jesus took the disciples aside to speak with them privately. Of course what was on His mind was the sacrifice He was about to make for the sins of the human race.

The additional information provided in this Passion announcement is that the leaders of the Jews (the Sanhedrin) would condemn Jesus to death and then turn Him over to the Gentiles (Romans) for execution. The manner of His death is also specified: crucifixion—a Roman, not a Jewish, method of execution. And prior to His crucifixion would come cruel mocking and beating. But as in the other predictions, His resurrection on the third day was assured. The striking fact about these announcements is that the death of Christ was no accident. The "Lamb slain from the foundation of the world" (Rev. 13:8) willingly sacrificed Himself according to a divine plan and timetable.

C. Presumption and Persistence (20:20-34)

1. *Chief places in the kingdom* (20:20-28). It seems almost inconceivable that after another Passion announcement and teaching on humility (becoming as children), the disciples could be concerned about chief places in the kingdom. But we stand on the other side of the Cross and have the benefit of a written New Testament. The disciples' minds

were filled with a purely political concept of the messianic kingdom, and their spiritual sensitivities were blinded to what was going on around them (Luke 18:34).

It seems that the mother of James and John was the instigator of the request that her sons should sit at Jesus' right and left in the kingdom. If she (Salome) was the sister of the Virgin Mary (as seems likely from a comparison of Matt. 27:56; Mark 15:40-41; and John 19:25), her sons would have been cousins of Jesus; and her request that her sons have a privileged place in the kingdom was a natural one. Furthermore, Salome would not have been familiar with the concepts that Jesus had been trying to get across to the disciples. Her ambition was detached from their experience of deeper-life teaching.

As is clear from the parallel passage in Mark 10:35-45, James and John made the actual request for favored postions. In response, Jesus said that they did not realize what they were asking. Their misconception of the kingdom led them to seek the glory without enduring the suffering. Then He asked, "Are you able to drink the cup I am going to drink?" "To drink" is to accept or imbibe or endure; "the cup" refers to His suffering (Matt. 26:39,42; John 18:11).

The brothers' affirmative answer proved more fully that they had no idea of what Jesus was talking about. No mere sinless mortal could become the suffering substitute for all humanity and thereby achieve pardon for their sin. They committed themselves in a burst of loyalty: "We are able." Since the pair evidently was not ready for further explanation at the moment, Jesus simply informed them that they would indeed drink the cup. As a matter of fact, James became the first apostle to suffer martyrdom (Acts 12:2) and John later in life was exiled for his Christian witness to the Isle of Patmos, where he received the vision of the Revelation. Positions in the kingdom were not Jesus' to give but would be appointed by the Father.

Soon the rest of the disciples appeared on the scene and discovered what was going on. They were "indignant," no doubt because they wanted the chief places for themselves. At once Jesus intervened in the squabble and used it as a teaching opportunity. "Rulers of the Gentiles," who follow the worldly principles of greatness, "exercise lordship" from above. Among members of the kingdom, however, the principle is reversed. "Whoever wishes to be great among you must be your servant" (*diakanos*, from which we get the word deacon). "Whoever wishes to be first among you shall be your slave," taking the lowest position of all and giving up his rights in order to serve others.

The messianic King Himself is the most illustrious example of the principle just enunciated. "The Son of man," God's incarnate Son, voluntarily "came," "not to be served," not to lord it over others, "but to serve," to give Himself in serving others, "and to give [voluntarily] His life as a ransom [price paid to win release of one held in bondage] in place of many." One of the most magnificent passages on the humble service of Christ is Philippians 2:1-11.

2. *Healing two blind men* (20:29-34). As Jesus and His disciples crossed the Jordan and traveled toward Jerusalem, they took the usual route through Jericho. Along the way a crowd of Passover pilgrims joined them, and at Jericho the healing of two blind men occurred. This miracle is fittingly reported here because it illustrates again the Son of man's ministering and because the blind men showed some recognition of Jesus' messiahship (calling Him "Son of David"), significant as He headed toward the Cross.

When this account is placed alongside that of Mark 10:46-52 and Luke 18:35-43, differences occur which critics have sought to use to prove contradictions in the Bible. Especially noteworthy is the fact that Matthew and Mark report the miracle took place as Jesus was going out of Jericho and Luke as He was drawing near it. Matthew says there were two blind men while Mark and Luke mention only one. Probably the difference in number is to be accounted for by the fact that Matthew gives the fuller account while the other two gospel writers concentrate on the vocal member of the pair.

Probably the best way of explaining the difference in location is this. Jesus had passed through Jericho and had received no invitation to spend the night. On the other side of town He met Zacchaeus and brought him to faith in Himself and then returned with him to spend the night at the publican's house (Luke 19:1-9). As they returned to Jericho, the healing took place. It occurred, then, after Jesus had passed through Jericho but was on His way back into town. Thus one may view the miracle as having taken place on the way into or out of Jericho.

"Lord, Son of David, have mercy on us!" (NIV), the blind men called. The callous crowd, accustomed to the sight of blind beggars in a society where there were no social programs to help them, tried to quiet the nuisance. But the men would not be silenced. And Jesus chose to notice their pleas and to accept an ascription of messiahship before the whole crowd. Never before had He been willing to accept this recognition in public; now, just before the Crucifixion, it was time to do so. Jesus healed the men and evidently bestowed on them salvation of soul as well (Mark 10:52). And they followed Jesus and continued to give Him praise (Luke 18:43).

For Further Study

1. With the help of a concordance, make a study of the occasions when Jesus took special interest in children.

2. According to the New Testament, what sort of heavenly rewards can believers expect for faithfulness in service?

3. Compare all Jesus' miracles of healing the blind in terms of their appeal, His method, and their response.

Chapter 11

Messiah's Rejection by the Jewish Leaders
(Matthew 21:1–23:39)

A. Reception in Jerusalem (21:1-27)

1. *The triumphal entry into Jerusalem* (21:1-11). The week had finally arrived for which Jesus had been born—the week in which He would bear the penalty of sin for the human race. He would begin the week with an assertion of His messiahship and His triumphal entry into Jerusalem and end it as the resurrected Lord of glory. As is clear from the Gospel of John (12:1, 12-15), the triumphal entry occurred on the Sunday before Easter. John also supplies the information that Jesus spent Saturday at Bethany and that popular fervor had been whipped up by the raising of Lazarus. Bethany, the home of Mary, Martha, and Lazarus and Jesus' headquarters during the first part of Passion week, is about two miles east of Jerusalem on the eastern slope of the Mount of Olives. Bethphage has completely disappeared but is thought to have been on the western slope of the mount.

After Jesus and His disciples had left Bethany on that Sunday morning and had drawn near Bethphage, Jesus sent two of the disciples into Bethphage with specific instructions. Who the two were is not stated, and it cannot be deduced from a comparison of parallel passages in the Gospels. They were told that just inside the village they would find a donkey and her colt tied up. They were to loose them and bring them to Jesus. If they were stopped, they were to say that the Lord needed them; and as Mark noted, He would return them shortly (Mark 11:3).

Several observations are in order at this point. First, Jesus planned to ride the colt into Jerusalem; unused animals were regarded as especially suited to sacred purposes. Second, Jesus wanted the mother to accompany the colt so it would behave in docile fashion. Third, Jesus must have been known to the owners for them to have so readily granted the request. Fourth, the omniscience of Jesus is indicated by His statement of where the animals were and the specific nature of the conversation concerning them. It seems clear that as Jesus prepared to ride into Jerusalem He intended to fulfill the messianic prophecy of Zechariah 9:9, but He did not make a point of the matter with the disciples or the crowd.

The two disciples experienced everything exactly as Jesus had said they would. Of course they found the colt without a saddle; so they threw their outer cloaks on its back for Jesus to sit on. As He moved forward many spread cloaks and tree branches on the dusty road to "pave" it and to prevent a cloud of dust from enveloping the Master. As a matter of fact, there were two crowds. One accompanied Jesus and largely surrounded Him. A second crowd gathered in Jerusalem when they heard that Jesus had left Bethany and was on the way to the city. They went forth to meet Jesus, carrying palm branches as they went. Evidently the two groups met on the slope of the Mount of Olives (John 12:12-13; Luke 19:37) and began the chant recorded in verse 9.

"Blessed is he who comes in the name of the Lord" is quoted from Psalm 118:26 and is part of the *Hallel* sung especially at Passover. From the passages in the four Gospels it is clear that the crowd hailed Jesus as Son of David and King of Israel and thus extended to Him a degree of messianic recognition. But this understanding was minimal because when inhabitants of Jerusalem later asked the crowds, "Who is this?" they answered, "Jesus, the prophet from Nazareth" (NIV). They did not call Him the Messiah.

The two crowds escorted Jesus down the slope to the Mount of Olives, across the Kidron, and to Jerusalem, where the inhabitants were profoundly stirred by this event. Although the Pharisees viewed this popular demonstration as a threat to the religious establishment (John 12:19), the Romans did not seem to have considered it to be anything more than a religious event connected with the Passover season. Soon the excitement was over, and Jesus and the disciples made a private tour of the temple and returned to Bethany for the night (Mark 11:11).

2. *Jesus in the temple* (21:12-17). As is clear from the Gospel of Mark, where the approach is chronological, Jesus made His triumphal entry into Jerusalem on Sunday afternoon and subsequently made a quick visit to the temple, observing the activity going on there but doing

nothing about it at such a late hour. Then He returned to Bethany for the night. On Monday morning He cursed the fig tree on the way into the city, apparently spent a good part of the day in the temple, and returned to Bethany for the night. On Tuesday morning the fig tree was already withered. Matthew, with his topical approach, often ignored minor details and was not always concerned with the chronology. He separately took up the triumphal entry, the cleansing of the temple, and the cursing of the fig tree.

Worshipers who came to the temple from a distance had to buy sacrificial animals and birds locally. Moreover, those who came from many lands had to get their currency changed into the sacred shekels so they could pay their temple tax. The sons of Annas, including Caiaphas, the reigning high priest, had established booths for moneychangers and the sale of birds and animals in the court of the Gentiles in the temple. Both the noise and confusion in a sacred place and the extortionate rates charged were reprehensible. Jesus overturned the low tables of the moneychangers, behind which they sat on the ground, and the benches of those who sold doves and expelled all those engaged in commercial dealings.

As He did so, Jesus made the astounding claim: "My house"—equating Himself with God—"shall be called a house of prayer." Clearly He was stating a messianic claim. Moreover, He was throwing His weight behind the inspiration of the Old Testament: "It stands written." Then He pronounced judgment on the evil priests: "You are making it a 'den of robbers.'" The first part of His statement is from Isaiah 56:7 and the latter part from Jeremiah 7:11. As Jesus asserted His authority, no members of the priestly establishment opposed Him as they had when He cleansed the temple at the beginning of His ministry three years earlier (John 2:13-22). In fact, they even stood by silently while He performed numerous miracles of healing. They did not dare seize Him or oust Him in the presence of Passover pilgrims who evidently were favorable to Him.

But when some boys began chanting, "Hosanna [praise, hail] to the son of David," and thus ascribed messianic status to Him, that was too much. Even then, however, the religious leaders could do no more than remonstrate with Him. Far from reproving the boys, Jesus quoted Psalm 8:2. If grown men would not respond, God "will perfect praise" for Himself "out of the mouths of little children and babies." Jesus did not consider them too young to know what they were doing, as the priests had intimated; He accepted their messianic ascriptions. And in quoting this passage from the Psalms, He was claiming to be God, the Messiah, David's Son. With that, Jesus turned His back on the rulers of the Jews and left Jerusalem to spend the night at Bethany, presumably again at the house of Mary and Martha and Lazarus.

3. *The withered fig tree* (21:18-22). As already noted, on Monday morning Jesus cursed a fig tree on His way into Jerusalem. Hungry, He had gone up to a fig tree; but finding no fruit on it, He cursed it so it would not bear fruit again. The curse was no act of personal indignation because it was not even the season when ripe figs could be expected (Mark 11:13). Jesus should have found evidence of fruit, however, because figs normally came before leaves; so here was a profession of fruitfulness but no real fruit.

Judgment on the tree must be interpreted as an act of symbolic judgment similar to that of some of the Old Testament prophets. In the Old Testament Israel often is likened to a fig tree and the destruction of a fig tree likened to judgment (e.g., Hos. 2:12; 9:10,16; Mic. 7:1-6). Here unbelieving Judaism is blasted by the judgment of God. Struck dead by the word of Jesus, the tree soon began to dry up from the roots (Mark 11:20).

On Tuesday morning the disciples were astonished by the rapidity of the tree's death and the evidence of Christ's power over nature. In response to the disciples' question as to "how" this happened, Jesus called attention to the source of the power demonstrated (God) and the means of tapping that source of power (faith). The message of verses 21 and 22 is similar to that of Matthew 17:20.

4. *The question of Jesus' authority* (21:23-27). On Tuesday, after the withered fig tree incident, Jesus went to the temple for His third visit in as many days. There He engaged in an extensive teaching ministry. At the close of one of His sessions, the chief priests and elders came to interrogate Him. In effect, they asked Him what kind of authority He possessed and who gave it to Him. "These things" would include His teaching, cleansing the temple on the previous day, and other aspects of His ministry. The Sanhedrin were not seeking information. They knew what authority Jesus claimed and would not accept it; to do so would result in their accepting Him as Messiah. They only wanted to get Him to state His claims so they could deny Him His authority. Hopefully He would express Himself in such a way as to trap Himself in some misstatement.

Jesus replied with a counterquestion, one that would at the same time expose their dishonesty and give them another chance to realize their blindness and to turn from it. In asking whether John's baptism (ministry) came from "heaven" or from "men," Jesus was virtually claiming that His authority stemmed from the same source as that of John the Baptist—His forerunner. The Sanhedrin did not dare to say John's authority came from heaven because then they should have believed him; nor did they dare to assert it was of human origin because they feared the excitable Passover crowds who believed John had the touch of God upon him. They preferred to plead ignorance—and to look ridiculous. Their dishonesty had been unmasked and they had refused another opportunity to turn from their spiritual perversity. They deserved no further answer.

B. Pointed Parables (21:28–22:14)

1. *Parable of the two sons* (21:28-32). Jesus next delivered three parables which further unmasked or castigated or pronounced judgment on the leaders of the Jews. And they were present for the action. A man had two dear sons and he went to each in turn asking him to work in his vineyard on a given day. The first brusquely refused but repented of his filial waywardness and went to work. The second gave an initially favorable response but later reneged. When asked which did the will of his father, the Sanhedrinists were forced to answer, "The first."

After Jesus had gotten the Sanhedrinists to condemn themselves, He proceeded to nail down the application. In the vineyard of Judaism two brothers were asked to respond to the message of John the Baptist: "the way of righteousness." The first, the publicans and harlots, as sinners, initially rejected his message; but later many of them received it. The second, the Pharisees and others, initially were somewhat positive (John 5:35) but later rejected him. It must have curdled the blood of the self-righteous Pharisees to be faced with the fact that they were brothers in perversity with the despised publicans and harlots, but "all have sinned and come short of the glory of God" (Rom. 3:23). Working in the vineyard was not a way of earning salvation because entrance into the kingdom clearly is based on *belief* in or acceptance of the message of John (v. 32). Of course the ministry of John was preparatory to that of Jesus. The next two parables put the rulers of the Jews in opposition to Jesus Himself.

2. *Parable of the wicked tenants* (21:33-46). Perhaps the rulers of

the Jews had heard enough, but Jesus detained them for further warning and condemnation. A landowner (God) planted a vineyard (Israel), leaving out nothing for its proper establishment. He not only planted the vineyard but surrounded it with a wall and provided it with a watchtower for its protection. Then he cut a winepress in the rock floor so the grapes could be crushed at harvest for their juice. Finally he leased the vineyard to vine growers (rulers of Israel) and went some distance away. The tenant farmers were expected to pay a certain percentage of the crop to the landlord at each harvest. At the background of the parable is Isaiah 5. There all Israel was guilty before God for their failure; here the rulers of Israel are guilty.

Periodically the owner sent out "slaves" (the prophets) to receive his share of the crop. Instead of rendering fruits of contrition and trust, the keepers of the vineyard roughly handled the slaves. One they beat to a bloody pulp, a second they simply murdered, a third they stoned like a common criminal. As time went on the owner sent many others to collect his due, with the same result of beatings and killings. No Jewish landowners would have put up with such treatment, but the patience of God did not wear thin; He continued to send His servants. "Last of all," as an ultimate appeal to the vine growers, the landlord sent his son. But they plotted among themselves to kill him so they could claim his inheritance. "They threw him out of the vineyard and killed him" are words that recall the crucifixion of Jesus outside the city of Jerusalem.

The reference is clear; the Jewish leaders found Jesus to be an obstacle to their control over Israel and were determined to kill Him so they could preserve their hold on the Jews. In fact, this very Sanhedrin, whom Jesus was addressing, had been plotting to kill Him ever since the raising of Lazarus (John 11:47-53). But He unmasked them and publicly revealed their plot, of course without mentioning any names.

At this juncture Jesus evidently asked the crowd what the landowner would do to those tenants. They replied with indignation as if this were a story from real life: "In vengeance he will put the scoundrels to death and rent the vineyard to other tenants who will promptly pay him the rent" (Williams). Jesus accepted their verdict and went on to quote a confirming prophecy from Psalm 118:22-23.

The application is clear: "The stone [Christ] which the builders [the Jewish leaders involved in constructing the old order] rejected [because it did not pass their tests] has now become the corner, binding together two adjoining walls in a whole new structure (church or new covenant).

In judgment God will take the kingdom from the Jews and give it to "other tenants" or "a people [nation] who will produce fruit." Reference is of course to the church which Peter called "an holy nation" in a context where he quoted the same Psalm 118 reference (1 Peter 2:9). The high priests and the Pharisees got the point. But instead of stopping to consider the warning and the prediction, they were stirred with anger and would have seized Jesus were it not for their fear of the pilgrims thronging the temple.

3. *The wedding guests* (22:1-14). Aware of what was going through the minds of His opponents, the omniscient Jesus "answered" their thoughts "in parables," or perhaps "in parabolic speech." It is not certain how many parables Jesus spoke on this occasion; Matthew records three, Mark only one. Luke's parable about a marriage feast (14:16-24) is not another version of this parable; numerous differences in detail lead to the conclusion that it was spoken on another occasion to teach different aspects of truth.

The history of "the kingdom of heaven may be compared to a king, who gave a wedding feast for his son" (NASB). The history of the kingdom from Jesus' first coming until the establishment of His messianic reign is compressed into this story about wedding guests. The king evidently is God the Father; the son, Jesus Christ; and the wedding feast, the offer of the grace of God to sinful humanity. The marriage of Yahweh to His people Israel was a concept familiar to Jewish ears and appeared several times in the Old Testatment.

Wedding guests received advance invitations and, in true Palestinian fashion, a second call at the time of the wedding feast, when "everything is ready." Probably the advance invitation came through Old Testament prophets, but Israel was "unwilling to come" (NASB). By an act of the will the guests rejected the grace of God extended to them. Then when "everything is ready," perhaps when Christ had come and had been crucified, raised, and ascended, they again received an invitation to accept God's grace (cf. 1 Cor. 5:7-8). This time some were merely indifferent, materialistically motivated; they centered their affections on their estates and commercial enterprises instead of on God and His concerns. Some were downright vicious; they persecuted and even killed the "slaves" of God, disciples, and others as they preached the gospel (e.g., Stephen, Acts 7:59; James, Acts 12:2).

Finally God brought judgment on the Jews for their opposition to Him. Verse 7 must be viewed as a prediction of the destruction of

Jerusalem in A.D. 70. The Roman army under Titus can be viewed as "his army," though pagan, because they accomplished His purposes. It is no more out of place for God to view the Roman army as "his army" than to classify pagan Nebuchadnezzar of Babylon as "my servant" (Jer. 25:9) or Cyrus of Persia as "his anointed" to do His will (Isa. 45:1).

The wicked rejection of the king's gracious invitations rendered the people (Jews) "unworthy"; so the king bid his servants to issue a general invitation to any who would come to the feast. "Be going," continue to go, to the "intersections" of roads so all travelers will be reached, the king commanded. "Bad and good" includes the morally upright and open sinners—all are in need of salvation and none can effect their own. Many view this invitation as involving a turning to the Gentiles, and it does include that; but it seems better to interpret it as a general invitation to Jews, Samaritans, and Gentiles (Acts 1:8).

When the king appeared before the assembled host, he spied one without a wedding garment. Evidently this garment was not finery provided by people who had come in off the street but was furnished by the king. It was a common practice in the ancient Near East for royalty to make gifts of clothing to people who appeared before them or served them. This practice is reflected in several passages of Scripture (e.g., Gen. 45:22; 2 Kings 10:22; Esth. 6:8-10; 8:15). Here reference must be to a robe of righteousness which God gives to those who trust Him fully for their salvation (see Isa. 61:10; Rev. 19:8-9). One who tries to come into the presence of the King on his own terms, who claims to be ready for the kingdom but is not (Isa. 64:6), will be cast out of the lighted palace and the presence of the King into the blackness of night—into the torments of hell. The call to accept the grace of God and attend the feast comes to all ("many are called") but few actually believe ("few are chosen," or elected to salvation).

C. Quarrelsome Questions (22:15-46)

1. *Question concerning taxation* (22:15-22). Jesus' warnings of personal and national judgment had no softening effect on the Pharisees. In fact, they became more determined than ever to dispose of Jesus. They "laid plans to trap him," as a hunter stalks his prey. The parallel account in Luke 20:20 notes that their plan was to involve Him in a charge of disloyalty or treason and to turn Him over to the Roman governor. The Pharisees themselves could not go to Jesus because they would be recognized. New faces and new tactics were needed. They decided to

send their disciples, carefully coached, and to team them up with the Herodians. Such strange bedfellows! The Pharisees hated any foreign domination and opposed paying taxes to a foreign power, though they did so; the Herodians, supporters of the Herodian family and Rome, would favor such payment of taxes.

The day was still Tuesday. The scene was still the temple. With flattering words the Pharisees' disciples sought to throw Jesus off guard. But more than that, their emphasis on His integrity and fearless devotion to the truth of God with no heed to the opinions of men was designed to force Him to face in a nonevasive way the issue they were about to raise. "Is it lawful [from a religious point of view] to pay the poll-tax to Caesar?" If He said yes, He would alienate the Pharisees and the Jews generally; if He said no, He would offend the Herodians and invite reprisals from the Roman authorities.

"Knowing their evil intent," both because of their evident trickery and His omniscience, Jesus unmasked the Pharisees' disciples on the spot. But He did not refuse an answer as He did when they had raised a question about John's baptism. Taking the offensive, Jesus told them to bring Him a denarius, the coin with which the poll tax was paid. This silver coin represented the daily wage of a laborer or soldier. Then He asked whose image and whose inscription were on the denarius. They answered, "Caesar's." This Caesar would have been Tiberius (who ruled A. D. 14-37), and the inscription would have claimed that he was the son of the divine Augustus and hence semi-divine himself. Then Jesus responded, "Give to Caesar what is Caesar's, and to God what is God's"(NIV).

In effect this statement says that Caesar has a right to mint coins, levy taxes, and govern; such acts do not infringe on the rights of God. One is obligated to pay for the benefits of Caesar's government. But Jesus' listeners also had obligations to God. His sharp distinction between the two spheres implied rejection of the idea that Caesar was divine, but it did not imply any necessary conflict between the two areas of responsibility. Again Jesus had silenced His questioners. "They were dumbfounded" (Williams) and went away.

2. *Question concerning resurrection* (22:23-33). But Jesus' opposition was not yet through with Him. A little later that same day a group of Sadducees came to question Him. The Sadducees, of the priestly class, would feel as threatened as the Pharisees by the successes of Jesus and the possibility that He might set up His kingdom. Influenced by the

nonsupernaturalism of Greco-Roman thought, they did not believe in
the resurrection of the body, the immortality of the soul, or the existence of angels and spirits. But they were firm adherents to the law of
Moses.

On this occasion the opposition decided to raise a question about
resurrection and tried to make the concept look ridiculous by treating it
in the most literal way so as to make Jesus look like a poor teacher. Verse
24 is a brief statement of the principle of levirate marriage (marrying the
childless wife of a dead brother in order to prevent his line from dying
out, cf. Deut. 25:5-10). The Sadducees erected a straw man by dragging
out the principle to apply to all seven brothers and then asked whose
wife she would be in the resurrection.

In His reply Jesus first stigmatized the Sadducees for failing to
understand either the tenor of the Scripture or the power of God. If they
properly understood the power of God, they would not have doubted
His power to raise the dead. They would have seen this problem in a
larger context of the whole spiritual world of which angels (which they
rejected) are a part. Marriage ceases to have any sexual importance in
heaven, and the resurrection life of men and women will be like that of
the angels; it will center on communion with God.

Next, in verses 31-32, Jesus proceeded to deal with the Sadducees'
failure to understand the tenor of Scripture. He reminded them of
Moses' experience at the burning bush when God told Moses, "I am the
God of Abraham, the God of Isaac, and the God of Jacob." And Jesus
concluded, "God is not the God of the dead, but of the living." In other
words, for God to say to Moses centuries after the death of the patriarchs, "I am the God of . . ." required that this fact still be true, that the
patriarchs were still alive in the invisible world.

"And when the crowds heard this, they were dumbfounded at His
teaching" (Williams). This must be a summary statement of the effect of
this episode. Many of these people were not present when Jesus talked
to the Sadducees or were too far away to hear what was being said. But
they heard the report of what He had said and "continued in a state of
amazement" at His teaching, which had so thoroughly refuted the
Sadducees.

3. *Question concerning the greatest commandment* (22:34-40).
When the Pharisees (supernaturalists, believers in a resurrection) saw
how Jesus had silenced their enemies the Sadducees (antisupernaturalists, opponents of resurrection), they got together and

agreed that one should be their spokesman in putting another question to Jesus. He, an expert in the law of Moses, sought to "test" Jesus or to try Him out on another question. Apparently the motive was not to snare Jesus because the questioner drew no rebuke but even a commendation from the Master (see Mark 12:28-34). Perhaps the lawyer's motive was twofold: to get some further pronouncement against the Sadducees and to find out which of the 613 individual statements the Pharisees had deduced from the law Jesus considered to be the weightiest. So he put his quesion: "What kind of commandment is first of all," i.e., was to be ranked in highest place. Would Jesus choose one of the 613 and thus support the Pharisees, or would He come down on the side of the Sadducees and declare that all these Pharisaic statements were mere traditions of the fathers?

As in other situations that would put Jesus in a bind or obligate Him to some human individual or group, Jesus chose a third position on this occasion. The greatest or first commandment, based on Deuteronomy 6:5, summarizes the first table of the Ten Commandments and in essence requires a love for God that dominates every area of one's being. The second, like it in nature and flowing from it, is based on Leviticus 19:18 and summarizes the second table of the law: "Love your neighbor as yourself." The meaning of "on these two commandments hangs the weight of all the law and the prophets" comes a little clearer in the Williams translation: "The essence of the whole law and the prophets is packed into these two commands." In other words, one should not view the law in a legal way. The real concern of the law and the prophets was not some external code of conduct but one's inner spiritual condition. Love for God and man on this plane was impossible by means of pure human effort. The grace and power of God working in the individual life were as necessary under law as they are under gospel.

4. *Paradoxical question about David's Son* (22:41-46). While the Pharisees were still standing around, Jesus had a question for them. Evidently He asked it, not to belittle or scold them in any way, but to encourage greater recognition of Himself. "What is your opinion of the Christ [Messiah?] Whose son is He?" (Williams). Without a moment's hesitation, they replied, "David's." It did not take doctors of the law to answer such a question. The pilgrims had cried it on Sunday and children had aped their elders in the temple courts on Monday.

Next Jesus alluded to Psalm 110, which Jews recognized as messianic and Jesus declared to be of Davidic authorship and given by divine inspiration (cf. Mark 12:36). David called this descendant his "Lord" or superior and went on to say, in the words of Psalm 110:1, "The Lord [Yahweh, God the Father] said to my Lord [Adonai, the Messiah, clearly also divine], 'Sit at My right hand [take the place of honor in heaven itself], Til I put your enemies under your feet' [until opposition is quelled and Christ returns to sit on the throne of David on earth]." How can Messiah be David's son if David calls Him Lord? If He is to be David's Lord, He had to be more than a man; He had to be a member of the Godhead.

"No one was able to answer him a word" because all refused to give the right answer. They refused to recognize Him as Messiah. And with the scribes and Pharisees still present, Jesus launched into a public denunciation of them.

D. Warnings and Woes (23:1-39)

1. *Warning concerning the Pharisees* (23:1-12). The scribes were the lawyers or legal experts among the Pharisees; and though distinguished from the larger group, they were part of it. Beck's identification of the scribes as "Bible scholars" alludes to the larger scope of their ministry. To say the Pharisees "sit in Moses' seat" means "they occupy Moses' position among you as expounders of the Law" (Kent, p. 970). Because they taught the injunctions of God as recorded in inspired Scripture, they were to be obeyed. "Do everything they say" must mean "everything they say that is of divine origin." Jesus clearly did not and could not endorse everything the Pharisees taught. In fact, earlier He had warned against their false teachings (Matt. 16:11-12).

"But stop doing what they do" is an injunction for the common people to stop following the example of the Pharisees, "for they do not practice what they preach" (NIV). In their hypocrisy they practiced a mere religious externalism and actually violated the clear intent of the Word by their traditions; "they abused the law by their rank work-righteousness" and "they missed its supreme purpose: the knowledge of sin and true contrition" (Lenski, p. 895). Verse 4 is commonly interpreted to refer to the Pharisees' multitudinous additions to the law.

In verses 5-7 Jesus elaborated on Pharisaic hypocrisy. Instead of being truly interested in honoring God, they really wanted human honors. They broadened their "phylacteries." These were small cases, containing pieces of parchment bearing Exodus 13:3-17; Deuteronomy 6:4-9; 11:13-21, fastened to the left wrist and the forehead in accordance with a literal interpretation of Exodus 13:16. In broadening these, the Pharisees made them as prominent as possible to give themselves an appearance of greater piety. Likewise for show they lengthened the tassels on the four corners of their outer robe (Num. 15:38; Deut. 22:12). And they loved the place of honor at banquets and the chief seats in the synagogues, raised seats facing the congregation, where they could be clearly seen. Moreover, they loved the deference paid them in public and the greeting of "Rabbi," great one—equivalent to teacher or doctor and signifying a spiritual instructor.

With Pharisaic activity Jesus contrasted Christian conduct. "You are not to be called 'Rabbi' [teacher], for one is your teacher and you are all brothers." There are, of course, divinely appointed officers in the church, and teacher is one of these (Eph. 4:11; 1 Cor. 12:29). But the human teacher is not to assume an authority or autocracy that sets aside the leadership or instructional directives of Christ in the church or the equality of all believers before God. In verse 9 the point seems not to be a prohibition against calling one a father in the faith, for Scripture itself alludes to such paternal relationships (1 Cor. 4:15,17; 1 Tim. 1:2). It means, rather, that a human father-figure does not have authority to make us do something contrary to the Word of God; there is only one Father over us all.

Verses 11 and 12 help to make clear the teaching of verses 8-10. While one may be a teacher, or a highly revered father-figure or some other kind of leader in the church, his desire should not be to lord it over others but to render humble service, giving due recognition to the headship of Christ, the authority of the Word of God, and the need for divine wisdom in interpreting the Word of God, and fulfilling one's duties.

2. *Woes on the Pharisees* (23:13-36). Jesus turned His attention from the disciples and spoke directly to the Pharisees, pronouncing a series of seven woes upon them. These are not curses or predictions but statements of fact. Of course not all the Pharisees were the brunt of the many condemnations uttered here or elsewhere in the Gospels, for a few responded to Jesus' messianic claims.

1. By your legalism, self-righteousness, and refusal to accept Jesus' messianic claims, "you yourselves do not enter" the kingdom. And worse, "you bolt the doors of the kingdom of heaven in men's faces" (Williams) by false teaching and hypocritical practices. Verse 14 is not in the better Greek manuscripts.

2. Though you prevent people from entering the kingdom of heaven, you spare no effort to make proselytes—converts of Gentiles to Judaism. Such converts are "twice as much a son of Gehenna as you are." This is so because "those who exchange one religion for another are more likely to show an intemperate zeal for their new religion, than those who have experienced no such dramatic change. So the converts of the Pharisees tended to become even more Pharisaic than the Pharisees themselves" (Tasker, p. 220). "Sons of Gehenna" were those worthy of being cast into Gehenna (hell, the place of the accursed) in the afterlife. If the proselyte is twice as much a son of Gehenna as the scribes and Pharisees, then the scribes and Pharisees are also "sons of Gehenna."

3. Verses 16-22 condemn the scribes and Pharisees for their subtle distinctions as to the sanctity of oaths. By their false argumentation they had virtually destroyed the sanctity of oath taking. With all solemnity they would make oaths that to the other party appeared to be binding, but the Pharisees had certain kinds of mental reservations which made the oath mean "nothing." They were "blind guides" because of their willful ignorance and perversion of truth and "fools" because anyone with common sense should be able to see that the greater includes the lesser. Thus the temple is greater than the gold in it, the altar than the sacrifice upon it, and God than heaven. The fact that the Pharisees' senseless distinctions had made a mockery out of oath taking was one reason why Jesus had said earlier, "Do not swear at all" (Matt. 5:33-37).

4. Next Jesus scored the Pharisees for their hypocrisy in giving careful attention to minor features of the law but neglecting the essential elements (vv. 23-24). In line with Leviticus 27:30, they were scrupulous in tithing (giving a tenth) even the most insignificant herbs: "mint," "dill" (used as a sedative and for cooking), and "cummin" (a spice used in breads and stews). But they "left out" or "dismissed," the vital require- ments of the law: "to be just, merciful, and trustworthy" (Beck)—to be characterized by righteous judgment, the showing of mercy, and trustworthiness or faithfulness. These major things were required but the others were also expected. By their conduct of majoring on the minors, these blind men who pretended to show others the way were so ridiculous that they appeared to be straining out the smallest Levitically unclean insect, the gnat, from their food but gulping down the camel, the largest Levitically unclean animal in Palestine (Lev. 11:4).

5. The fifth woe (vv. 25-26) castigated the Pharisees for their attention to the externals of religion, particularly for rabbinical or

ritualistic purification of vessels from which they ate their expensive food, while they "disregarded the manner in which they secured the wealth from which they feasted" (Lenski, p. 901). "Within they are full from extortion and excess" (ASV) is more effectively translated "full of produce gained by sweated labour and profiteering" (Tasker, p. 221). Then to make the condemnation personal, Jesus used the singular and urged inner moral cleanness which will result in an external cleanness that is genuine rather than a mere hypocritical façade.

6. The sixth woe (vv. 27-28) in essence says, "Woe unto you because, like whitewashed tombs, you appear beautiful on the outside. That is, you appear to be righteous, but inside you are full of bones of dead men, full of moral corruption or spiritual death." Jesus' analogy may have been drawn from the fact that annually before Passover Jews whitewashed tombs to make them clearly identifiable so no one would touch them and become Levitically unclean. Or it may have risen from the fact that expensive tombs were adorned with ornamental lime plaster to make them appear more beautiful.

7. Last (vv. 29-36), Jesus pronounced a woe on the Pharisees who thought they had identified themselves with the ancient prophets by building ornate martyr memorials over their graves and by declaring they would never have participated in the shedding of their blood if they had lived then. Actually they were bearing witness against themselves that they were descendants of those murderous persons by their impenitence and failure to heed the call of the prophets to lives of genuine faith and devoid of hyprocritical sham. Moreover, they were descendants of those earlier murderers by their intent to destroy Jesus (Matt. 21:46). And in words almost anticipatory of what He would say to Judas (John 13:27), Jesus said to the Pharisees, "Go on, finish what your fathers started" (Beck).

Not only would the Pharisees try to destroy Jesus, but they and other Jewish leaders would also persecute and kill other servants of God (apostles and others) who would come along in the early church (v. 34). And in fact punishment for the sins of the fathers was about to fall on the Jewish nation for all the shedding of righteous blood, from the killing of Abel (Gen. 4:8) to the killing of Zacharias (2 Chron. 24:20-22), that is, from the beginning of the Hebrew Bible to the end of it. The Hebrew Bible has an order different from the English and gives 2 Chronicles last. The judgment would, of course, result in the destruction of Jerusalem.

For elucidation of "offspring of vipers" (v. 33), see comments on Matthew 3:7.

3. *Lament over Jerusalem* (23:37-39). Into the context of stern denunciation Jesus introduced a note of tenderness. With a breaking heart He lamented over the city and nation that refused Him and His message. As He left the temple for the last time before His crucifixion, Jesus said, "Your house is being abandoned by me" (Williams). It was no longer God's house but theirs. His ministry was coming to an end, and the Jews as a people would not see Him again until His second coming, when they would recognize and accept their Messiah (Zech 12:10).

For Further Study

1. Read articles on the Pharisees, Sadducees, and Herodians in a good Bible encyclopedia or Bible dictionary.

2. What does it mean to "love your neighbor as yourself"? What does it mean to love yourself?

3. Try to make a list of teachings and practices of the Pharisees which would "bolt the door of the kingdom of heaven in men's faces."

4. Tabulate or summarize the approaches used by the various opponents of Jesus in this chapter to trap Him.

Chapter 12

Messiah's Revelation Concerning the Future
(Matthew 24:1–25:46)

A. End-time Events (24:1-31; 25:31-46)

1. *Occasion for the Olivet Discourse* (24:1-3). Soon after Jesus' lament over Jerusalem (Matt. 23:37-39), He left the temple with His disciples and walked toward Bethany. Ringing in the disciples' ears as they went were the words of Jesus declaring His abandonment of the temple and its desolation (23:38). This declaration seems to have given rise to a certain sadness or reflection about this marvelous collection of structures on which Herod the Great and his successors had been expending so much wealth and energy for almost fifty years. As the disciples called Jesus' attention to the magnificence of the temple complex, He startled them by predicting its utter destruction. Presumably they were too stunned to ask questions—especially in front of crowds of Passover pilgrims.

But after they had crossed the Kidron Valley and had climbed the Mount of Olives to the east, Jesus sat down near the brow of the hill and the disciples had a chance to ask Him some questions privately. "When will this happen, and what will be the sign of your coming and of the end of the age?" (NIV). They were not asking for a specific date. "When" should be linked to the request for a "sign" that would indicate the nearness of Jesus' return to exercise judgment and to bring to an end the present age. Their questions rose from the common Jewish interpretation of the Old Testament that viewed the coming of Messiah as bringing in a new age and as accompanied by a judgment. Whatever may have been their motivation in asking these questions or how much understanding they had of the prophetic future is almost irrelevant. The chief point to note is that the questions provided an occasion for Jesus' great

Olivet Discourse—so-called because He delivered it on the Mount of Olives. Jesus' reply failed to deal with the first question, which was answered in the destruction of Jerusalem in A.D. 70, but went on to comment on His second coming and the end of the age.

2. *Structure and interpretation of the Olivet Discourse.* Admittedly these two chapters are full of problems of interpretation, but even a cursory study reveals a clearly identifiable order of future events. To discover what Matthew was predicting, one probably should first get the background of 24:15. Daniel laid out an arrangement of seventy weeks of years (a week of seven days standing for seven years) which is to culminate in a seventieth week of tribulation. He stated clearly (Dan. 9:27) that at the beginning of the Tribulation a prince would make a covenant with the Jews. But in the middle of it he would break that covenant and would cause sacrifice to cease and an abomination of desolation (evidently some pagan altar or image) to be set up.

Clearly Matthew 24:15 and the parallel passage in Mark 13:14 delineate the middle of the Tribulation. At that point the Great Tribulation begins—the worst in the history of the world (Matt. 24:21). What appears before 24:15 must have something to do with the first half of the Tribulation (beginning of travail, 24:8). Following the last half of the Tribulation Christ will return (24:29-31). This is the same order of events predicted in Revelation, where the Tribulation is followed by the second coming of Christ (Rev. 19:11-21). After a statement about the Second Coming in Matthew 24:29-31, a long parenthetical section of parables and exhortation to watchfulness in view of Christ's return intervenes before the account of His return is resumed (25:31). At that juncture occurs a description of judgment: those judged worthy enter the kingdom.

3. *Beginning of birthpains* (24:4-14). It seems impossible to restrict these verses to a description of the first half of the Tribulation or to think of the predictions in them as specific signs of the return of Christ. These tragedies or evils have occurred throughout the present age, but apparently their increasing intensity portends the increasing imminency of Jesus' coming. And they will especially characterize the first half of the Tribulation. Jesus named a whole catalog of signs to watch: incidence of false christs (vv. 4-5); wars and rumors of wars (vv. 6-7); famines (v. 7); pestilence (v. 7); earthquakes (v. 7); martyrdoms (vv. 8-10); false prophets (v. 11); increasing lawlessness (v. 12); "crime wave" (Williams).

All these difficulties are considered to be the "beginning of birth-pangs" (v. 8). As in childbirth, such agonies will be followed by much more severe pains before deliverance occurs with the return of Christ in glory. Under such conditions it will be increasingly impossible to endure. "But he who stands firm [endures] to the end will be saved" (v. 13, NIV). This verse should not be considered as a means of salvation because salvation is accomplished through the grace of God, not through human effort. The context appears to be that of the Tribulation and the one who endures to the end of it will be saved.

Kent interprets, "But the distinguishing mark of the saved Jewish remnant will be their enduring in faith to the end" (p. 972). Walvoord concludes that the reference is to those who survive the Tribulation and are alive at Christ's coming; such will be delivered from their persecutors and will enter the kingdom. Many will not survive but will be martyred for their faith (p. 184). The "good news of the kingdom," the announcement of the coming Messiah and salvation through His provision, will be proclaimed throughout the world before Jesus' return.

4. *The Great Tribulation* (24:15-28). The signal for the onslaught of the terrible trials of the Great Tribulation and the end of the age will be the setting up of the "abomination of desolation" in the holy place, requiring of course the rebuilding of the temple. The "abomination" is an object that is detestable and in the Old Testament denoted idolatry or sacrilege (e.g., Deut. 29:16-17; 1 Kings 11:6-7). "Of desolation" indicates the effect produced: the "abomination that makes desolate." Probably reference is to the Antichrist who will set up his false worship in the temple (see discussion above on Daniel's Seventieth Week; cf. Mark 13:14; 2 Thess. 2:4).

When the abomination of desolation is installed, terrible persecution will descend on the Jews and extreme haste will be necessary to escape. The context is thoroughly Jewish and reminds us of the fact that the judgment of the Tribulation is especially against the Jews who had persistently rejected God and His servants the prophets and were now in the process of rejecting Jesus the Messiah. The mountain fastnesses of Judea have given refuge to many in flight from the days of David to those of Bar Kochba and since.

One who is doing something on the flat top of his house when the news is flashed should not even go inside to pick up any belongings; he should flee by the outside stairway. One who is working in the field should not go to his house to get his outer cloak. Especially to be pitied are expectant and nursing mothers whose condition will impede flight.

"Pray that your flight not be in winter," when the rains fill the wadis[1] in the Judean hills and swell the streams and hinder movement.

The Great Tribulation will be of unparalleled intensity. Verse 21 singles it out as the greatest tribulation of all time, undoubtedly the one referred to in the Book of Revelation and Daniel 12:1. In fact, it will be so severe that the population of the area would be wiped out "if those days had not been cut short," if God had not already decreed limits on the duration of the Tribulation. God set those limits for the sake of "the elect," true believers then living.

In the midst of all these trials false messiahs and false prophets will arise, no doubt promising to solve the problems or meet the needs of the hour. As credentials they will "show signs and wonders," either fabricating amazing things or by demonic activity actually performing miracles. The Revelation also predicts that demon-empowered persons will have miraculous power duing the Tribulation (Rev. 13:13-15; 16:14; cf. 2 Thess. 2:9-10).

Supernatural demonstrations do not prove that a ministry is of God. These false religious leaders will try to lead even true believers astray "if possible"; the inference is that such efforts will not be successful. Believers will know with assurance, however, whether or not a claimant is the Messiah, for the coming of the Son of man will be "as the lightning," with suddenness or swiftness, not with public preachments or extended claims. And it will be accompanied by fearsome natural phenomena. "Wherever there is a carcass, there the vultures will flock" (Williams) is a reference to the execution of divine judgment on moral corruption when Christ returns (Rev. 19:17-18).

5. *Return of Messiah* (24:29-31). "Immediately, after the tribulation," without an extended interval of time, shall appear a variety of cosmic disturbances which commentators often have treated as symbolizing political and international upheaval. But there is no reason why these predictions should not be taken literally. "The powers of the heavens will be shaken" (NASB) or dislocated, a divine disruption of the heavens will produce a terrifying cataclysm. "And then," immediately following, "the sign of the Son of man will appear," "the sign by which he shows his presence" (Lenski, p. 948), probably the blinding, dazzling glory which characterizes Him alone.

"All the tribes of the earth will mourn." Certainly all the Jews who

---

[1] A wadi is a stream bed that is dry most of the year but may become a raging torrent during the rainy season.

have rejected the Messiah, and other peoples as well, will be over-whelmed with grief and despair at the sight of the One whom they had despised and rejected. "On the clouds of the sky" probably refers not to natural clouds but something like the "cloud of the Presence" that descended on the tabernacle in the wilderness and led the Israelites on their wilderness wanderings (see Dan. 7:13-14). Or possibly they refer to clouds or hosts of glorified saints and angels. In any case, He will come "in overwhelming power and splendor" (Williams).

"All will see the Son of man." His return will be physical and visible and will involve an extended exposure to mankind. He will send out His angels to gather the elect from the remotest parts of the earth. Presuma-bly these are only believers living on earth at the time, Tribulation saints who "endured to the end" of the Tribulation. These elect evidently are the "sheep" at the judgment which immediately takes place. What is in view in these verses in a posttribulation return of Christ in judgment and has nothing to do with the question of a pretribulation rapture, which is not in view in Matthew 24–25.

6. *Judgment of the nations* (25:31-46). After having revealed what would befall the Jews at the end of the Tribulation, Jesus focused His attention on the Gentiles. When all nations will stand before the tri-bunal of Christ, "he will separate the people from one another." Judg-ment as individuals is required in the nature of the case because the acts of kindness or unkindness described are performed by individuals, and there never has been a righteous or "sheep" nation.

In this scene Christ clearly is the judge. Those placed on His right (the sheep) are the righteous and those on His left the unrighteous ("the goats"). The reward of the righteous is to enter the kingdom prepared for them from the creation of the world. In this context that would appear to mean they are to enter the millennial kingdom which is about to be set up on earth. The order of events is the same as in Revelation where in chapter 19 Christ comes at the end of the Tribulation and in chapter 20 He establishes the Millennium. The basis of the judgment is treatment of "my brethren" (v. 40).

The most natural interpretation of this passage would identify the "nations" as Gentiles and the "brethren" as Jews (Jesus' brethren after the flesh), who will be horribly persecuted during the Tribulation (24:9, 19-22). One might argue that Jesus' brethren included all believers (Matt. 12:47-50), but the context of Matthew 24–25 is strictly Jewish; and in the more general spiritual sense Jewish brethren will serve as missionaries, preaching the gospel of the kingdom to all the world during the Tribulation (24:14).

It is likely that persons who show kindness to Jewish missionaries or even to unbelieving Jews during the Tribulation will do so at the risk of their lives. And presumably such support or encouragement or protection will be extended only by believers and will be an evidence of their genuine faith. Jesus viewed these acts as done for the Messiah Himself (v. 40). Of course it may be argued that any believer's kindness to another believer during the Tribulation may be extended at the peril of his life and may be thought of as evidence of one's faith in Christ.

Conversely, those who do not receive the "brethren" are those who do not receive or support or encourage Jewish evangelists during the Tribulation or who do not accept the good news concerning the Messiah and His kingdom. Moreover, they do not protect other persecuted Jews or even persecuted Gentiles. The fact that they do none of these things is an indication of their lack of faith in Christ. Judgment is not so much for specific acts of commission or omission but the spiritual condition that these acts portray.

It is important to note that "everlasting fire" was not prepared for human beings but for "the devil and his angels" (v. 41), who have for many millennia set themselves against everything that God purposes and who constantly attempt to pull human beings away from faith in and service to God. "Eternal punishment" and "eternal life" (v. 46) are described in identical language in the Greek. There is no basis in Scripture for terminating punishment while continuing the fellowship of the blessed in heaven with God forever.

This judgment scene is not to be confused with the Great White Throne judgment of Revelation 20. Distinguishing features in the two events include the fact that in Matthew there is no evidence of a general resurrection (Rev. 20:13), the heavens and the earth have not passed away (Rev. 10:11), the Millennium has not occurred (Rev. 20:7), and the basis of judgment is different.

B. Applications and Illustrations of the Second Coming (24:32-25:30)

1. *The sprouting fig tree* (24:32-35). Some commentators take this fig tree to be symbolic of Israel, as it frequently is. If so, the rebirth of Israel would be a sign of the coming of Christ. It seems better to treat the tree as a literal tree and to note that as the budding of the fig tree indicates the coming of summer, so certain conditions will be sure signs

of Christ's return. "These things" (v. 33) which portend Christ's coming include intense earthquakes, famines, pestilence, the rise of false christs, and especially the Great Tribulation, at the beginning of which Daniel's "abomination of desolation" will appear.

"This generation" is frequently taken to refer literally to the generation to which Jesus was speaking. Such a view is possible only if one concludes that Jesus was horribly mistaken or that the announced prophetic scheme is not to be taken literally. The former is unthinkable and the latter subjects the prophetic message to human whim—permitting anyone to decide what is or is not to be fulfilled. In fact, verse 35 asserts the absolute certainty of the whole prophetic scheme and thus is a testimony to the inspiration of the Word and the sovereignty of God in controlling the movement of history. "Generation" also may be taken to refer to the Jewish race, which would be preserved until all these things are fulfilled—a powerful promise of God's continuing care of the Jews. Or perhaps the reference is to the generation of the end time. The generation that begins to see the budding of the fig tree, that begins to see definite signs of the Lord's coming, will not pass off the earth before all "these things" have occurred. That is, events will come in rapid succession and the time lapse involved will not be of extensive duration.

2. *Uncertain time of the coming* (24:36-51). Although there will be plenty of signs of Christ's return, no one knows the exact time of His appearance. In fact, "not even the Son" knows the exact time. Though these words do not appear in some Greek manuscripts and are omitted from the kjv, they have strong manuscript support and are included in most versions. Since infinite knowledge is an attribute or quality of deity, which all members of the Trinity share, one must conclude that ignorance of the time of His return was another of the limitations Jesus suffered in the humiliation of the Incarnation.

Just as signs of the second coming of Christ in judgment will point to the event, so signs of the coming of the Flood indicated nearness of that catastrophe. Noah preached and built but people went on about their business unheedingly. Even when Noah and his family went into the ark, the time of the Flood was evidently at hand but one could not assign an exact time. In fact, one cannot be sure of the exact hour of Christ's return until the event is in the process of occurring. And just as the coming of the Flood was a time of judgment ("took them all away," v. 39), so will be the coming of the Son of man.

"Then," at the time of His coming, two men may be working in the field or two women grinding at a handmill. In each case one will be taken and the other left. In the days of the Flood, the evil were removed and the just remained; at the posttribulation judgment the evil will be removed and cast into the lake of fire and the righteous will remain and go into the kingdom. The suddenness of His coming and the uncertainty of the time will require a life of expectancy on the part of the generation living at the end of the Tribulation: "So keep on watching, for you do not know on what day your Lord is coming" (Williams). Though the exhortation applies particularly to the days immediately after the Tribulation, it is pertinent to all believers who are enjoined to be ready for His imminent coming (1 Thess. 4:13-18).

Inability to determine the exact time of the Lord's return and thus the need for constant watchfulness is repeatedly emphasized in the Olivet Discourse (24:36,42,44,50; 25:13). But though the time of His coming may be uncertain, the fact of it is not; He "will come" (24:42,44,50; 25:31).

Next Jesus gave an illustration and a parable to underscore the need to "keep on watching" (v. 42). The owner of a house had a general idea of when a thief would break in (literally, *dig through* the mud-brick walls). But since he did not know in "what watch" of the night the robbery would occur, he grew careless and slept and was robbed. "So you, too, must continue to be ready" (Williams) because of the uncertainty of the time of His coming.

In the parable of the steward in the household (vv. 45-51), the faithful and wise steward, who was placed in charge of the other domestic servants, consistently did what his lord had instructed him to do. For his faithfulness the lord would reward him at his return. On the other hand, if a steward is "evil" and assumes "my master is not coming for a long time" (v. 48, NASB), he may cast off ethical and moral restraints and give vent to the baseness of his nature. The purifying effects of the lord's return have no effect on him and he becomes a tyrant and a confirmed worldling. But his unpreparedness for the momentary return of his lord does not alter the fact that such an evil person will be surprised by the lord's unexpected coming. Evidently he will not be judged as merely temporarily backslidden but will not even be classified as a believer. His conduct will be evidence of his true spiritual condition. Similarly, at Christ's return He will unmask such evil servants and cast them into perdition with other hypocrites.

3. *Parable of the ten virgins* (25:1-13). It is superficially obvious

that Jesus sought in this passage to teach the importance of watchfulness in the light of His return and that preparation should precede His return, not follow it. Several big questions remain however. Who are the virgins? On what basis are they judged? When does this judgment occur? What is its significance?

The following is offered as a tentative interpretation. The parable describes the judgment of Israel. The ten virgins refer to the professing remnant of Israel after the church has been taken up by the Rapture. The five wise virgins represent the believing remnant; the foolish, the unbelieving who profess to be looking for Messiah's coming in power. The marriage of the bridegroom to the bride has already occurred in heaven, and the parable alludes to the wedding feast which takes place on earth. The bridegroom's coming is the return of the Lord in glory at the end of the Tribulation. Entrance into the marriage feast corresponds to entrance into the kingdom of heaven on earth (the Millennium).

This interpretation may be defended on several bases. First, the Olivet Discourse tells of the Tribulation, Christ's coming at the end of it, and the judgment to follow, after which the blessed will enter the kingdom. The parables of these chapters serve to illustrate the main course of events. Matthew 24:27-51 describes what will happen at the end of the Tribulation. Matthew 25:1 begins with "then." So at the time of His coming after the Tribulation, the judgment of the ten virgins will occur.

Second, from the standpoint of Jewish marriage practices, it must be recognized that the marriage has already taken place and the bridegroom has gone to the home of the bride (the church) to claim her for himself and to bring her back to his home. The virgins are to join the procession on the way back to the bridegroom's house and are waiting at some intermediate place. To call Christ the bridegroom and the virgins the church (the bride), as many do, completely confuses the customary Jewish procedure. Some manuscripts add the words "and the bride" at the end of Matthew 25:1. Although those readings are inferior and incorrect, they at least indicate the interpretation held by some in the early church. This event takes place after the Rapture.

Third, the judgment of the virgins cannot have anything to do with the Rapture because in the clear references to the Rapture, believers are caught up to meet the Lord in the air. At that time there is no judgment of unbelievers as in verse 12; nor do they have access to Him as in verses 11-12.

Last, if the virgins are not the church, and if the judgment of Matthew 25:31-46 involves a judgment of Gentiles on the basis of their treatment of "my brethren" (more than likely Christ's brethren after the flesh—Jews), and since there is no other mention in this passage of the judgment of the Jews, what would be more likely than to find in this parable their premillennial judgment? The five wise virgins (representing regenerate Jews) then enter the Millennium along with righteous Gentiles vindicated in the judgment of Matthew 25. Though the interpretation of this passage seems to place its fulfillment some years in the future, the admonition to watchfulness is completely applicable to believers in the present day. Christ could return at any moment.

4. *The parable of the talents* (25:14-30). "Again, it will be like a man going on a journey" (NIV). Jesus' departure from the nation of Israel and His return to it again would be like a man going away on a long journey. Before going he turned over his property to his servants and on his return sought an accounting and rendered judgment. So this parable follows the same general theme as the last one—Jesus' return and the judgment He will render at that time. The master distributed "talents of money," silver talents in this case worth a minimum of $1,000 each in those days and infinitely more today. The uneven distribution is of gifts and responsibilities, "to each according to his ability," to each according to his capacity to function by virtue of natural endowments, educational opportunities, and the like. The sovereign Lord bestows on each what he should be able to handle.

The five-talent person proceeded without delay ("at once") to do the work of God, making 100 percent profit. The two-talent person did likewise. Both were faithful in their service and found ways of extending themselves and their ministry—through conversion of others, teaching others to teach others, organizing a group effort to achieve some goal, wise deployment of workers to achieve goals, and the like. The one-talent person was unfaithful. Though it was within his grasp to exercise his gifts and handle the responsibility incumbent upon him, he "hid his master's silver." He did not squander what God gave him, but by nonuse of his gift he lived as if he had none; and his unfaithfulness resulted in no expansion of the work of God whatsoever. Of course this passage does not teach that only a one-talent person may be unfaithful; those with many could be also.

On His return the Master will judge the faithfulness of His servants and will reward on that basis, not according to how many talents one possesses. The reward is threefold: (1) commendation: "Well done, good and faithful servant"; (2) elevation by Christ Himself: "I will put you in charge of many things"—perhaps a reference to some special position of authority in the kingdom (Millennium); (3) sharing in the heavenly joy of Christ Himself: "Come, share your master's joy" (Williams).

The unprofitable servant had a false view of his master, seeing him only as harsh or cruel instead of loving and generous. Out of a professed fear of his master he buried his talent in a safe place until the day of judgment. Perhaps verse 26 should be treated as a question: "Did you know that I reap?" Then why didn't you deposit my talent in the bank where it could draw interest? "The least we can do with Christ's gifts is to let others, who do business for the Lord on an extensive scale such as bankers do, use us and our small gifts in the Lord's work. Our gifts will then earn at least something" (Lenski, p. 984).

This faithless one lost his talent to one able to use it profitably and he was thrown into "outer darkness," eternal punishment. Evidently this is not merely a judgment of believers' works but must refer to a judgment of those who at the end of the Tribulation have no real faith in the Messiah. This parable must refer to the judgment of the sheep and goats at Jesus' return, the discussion of which begins in the very next verse. The one-talent person cast into "outer darkness" is identical with the goat who is thrown into "eternal fire" (v. 41).

This parable has a present application, which should in no way be confused with its interpretation. Those who are faithful in Christ's service are rewarded with greater responsibilities as they demonstrate that they can be trusted to do what has been assigned to them. Those who evidently cannot be counted on to do even minor tasks will lose the opportunity to perform at all. And persons who exercise their gifts discover that they develop significantly while those who do not exercise them find that they shrivel up completely.

For Further Study

1. Compare the account of Christ's return in Revelation 19 with that of the Olivet Discourse.

2. Compare the Great White Throne judgment of Revelation 20 with the judgment of Matthew 25.

3. Try to find another interpretation of the parable of the ten virgins in a commentary or a book on the parables.

4. Write a statement of how you could "invest" your talents.

Chapter 13

The Passion of the Messiah
(Matthew 26:1–27:66)

A. The Last Supper (26:1-35)

1. *God's timetable* (26:1-5). In the Olivet Discourse Jesus concentrated on events connected with His return. Though the predictions were frightful, they were in a sense reassuring, for they showed that the disciples' trust in the Messiah and their anticipation of His kingdom were not to be shattered by His departure. He had a sovereign plan and a timetable for accomplishing His purposes. This fact was further demonstrated by His announcement of the exact time of His betrayal for crucifixion: "after two days." It was then Tuesday, betrayal was to be on Thursday. And the divine timetable was set even though the Sanhedrin (chief priests and elders) planned to wait until the following week to seize Him, when the Passover pilgrims would no longer be in Jerusalem to come to His rescue (v. 3). Though they were quite firm in declaring Jesus' death would have to wait ("kept saying, 'It must not be at the feast'"), God's timing would prevail. The discussion of the Sanhedrin did not concern whether but how to take Him; the decision already had been made that He must die (John 11:50-52).

2. *Anointing of Jesus* (26:6-13). As is clear from the parallel account in John 12:1-11, this event took place on Saturday night before the triumphal entry. Jesus arrived at Bethany on Friday. No dinner could have been served that night because the Sabbath began at sundown; therefore it must have taken place on Saturday night after Sabbath was over. "Meanwhile" a crowd gathered in Bethany, when they learned of Jesus' presence, and "the next day" (Sunday) the triumphal entry occurred (John 12:9,12). This narrative is placed here, out of chronological order, because it helps to explain Judas' betrayal, which is described next.

171

Simon the Leper gave the dinner. Who he was we do not know, but certainly he was no longer a leper or he would not have been involved in such social affairs. Probably he was one of those whom Jesus had healed. The fact that Mary, Martha, and Lazarus figure so prominently in the account may indicate that Simon was their father. While the guests were reclining at dinner in the usual oriental fashion,[1] Mary came in with an alabaster flask of pure nard (ointment from India), poured the contents on His head and His feet, and then wiped His feet with her hair.

Judas immediately lost his patience and perhaps his temper (see John 12:4-6). Piously he protested such waste of perfume, worth 300 denarii, about a year's wages of a laborer, which might have been sold and the proceeds given to the poor. Actually as treasurer of the group who periodically embezzled funds, he had ulterior motives (see John 12:6). The other disciples followed his lead in scolding Mary (Matt. 26:8; Mark 14:4-5).

Jesus defended Mary, observing first that the poor are always present and can be helped at any time (Mark 14:7), but He would not always be present. Then He noted that this was an act of pure devotion signifying anointing for burial. This was a very striking pronouncement, which intimates that Mary may have been the only one to grasp the impact of Jesus' passion announcements and thus to understand what was really going on. Time spent in learning at His feet had given special insights (Luke 10:39,42). Then Jesus made the most startling pronouncement of all: "Wherever the gospel is preached in the whole world," this story of Mary's devotion would be told. At a moment when uncertainty and perhaps fear was beginning to grip the apostolic company as they braced themselves for the departure of Christ and the very real possibility that the movement He had launched might come to an abrupt halt, He declared that the good news would be preached in the whole world. What they were facing was not the end but only the beginning.

3. *Judas's betrayal* (26:14-16). "Then" evidently signals the fact that Judas's argument with Jesus at the dinner in Bethany was the breaking point in their relationship. Whatever dream he may have had of holding a high office in Messiah's kingdom had been dashed. It seemed clear to him that the end was near and he might as well salvage what he could for himself from the situation.

---

[1]Diners reclined on couches with their heads at the table, supported themselves on their left elbow, and ate with their right hand.

Judas made a contract for betrayal. Perhaps he broke in on the Sanhedrin during the meeting described in verses 3-5. The betrayal price of thirty pieces of silver cannot be computed positively. Not only is it impossible to discover what silver coin is meant, but it is also impossible to represent the amount meaningfully in current values. At the minimum it would be equivalent to the amount earned by a modern laborer in six weeks of employment. The price was the fulfillment of the prophecy in Zechariah 11:12-13 and may have been the price paid for a slave (Exod. 21:32; cf. Matt. 20:28; Phil. 2:7-8). Thereafter Judas sought an opportunity to fulfill his part of the bargain.

4. *The Passover* (26:17-25). Wednesday of Passion week is passed over in silence in all the Gospels. Apparently it was a day of rest for the Master and His disciples in preparation for momentous events about to occur. Evidently no plans had been announced for their Passover meal because on Thursday morning ("the first day of the Feast") they finally came to Him for instructions about where to prepare the Passover.

Actually only two disciples, Peter and John (Luke 22:8), went into Jerusalem with specific instructions to make the arrangements. The means by which they were to locate the man in whose house Jesus intended to eat the Passover meal are described in Mark 14:13. The statement to be made to him (Matt. 26:18) indicates that the man would be a disciple of Jesus rather advanced in the faith. He would be so well informed as to understand the message that "my time is near." The disciples followed instructions implicitly and prepared the Passover. This secrecy evidently was to prevent Judas from interfering with the divine timetable by informing the Sanhedrin where Jesus could be seized. To this day neither Scripture nor tradition provides the name of the man who so graciously provided for the apostolic company on this occasion.

When the group assembled and had nearly finished the meal, Jesus announced that one of the Twelve would betray Him. Immediately a pall of gloom settled over the gathering and one by one in rapid succession they asked, "It is not I, Lord, is it?" Verse 23 evidently was a private statement made to John alone and was meant to reveal to John the identity of the betrayer (see John 13:23-26). But Jesus was not at the mercy of a betrayer or a successful plot; His departure would be in fulfillment of Old Testament prophecy and according to divine plan. However, that fact will not exonerate the betrayer. His judgment was sure: "It would have been better for that man, if he had never been born!" (Williams). Then in response to Judas's question, Jesus told him that He knew that Judas was the betrayer and urged him to hurry up and do his dastardly deed. Judas went out into the night but the rest did not know why (John 13:27-30).

5. *Institution of the Lord's Supper* (26:26-30). During the course of the Passover meal, "as they were eating, Jesus took bread," the unleavened flat cakes that would have been on the table, "gave thanks," uttered a blessing over the bread, "broke it" for distribution and said to the disciples, "Take, eat; this is my body." Since He was still alive, He evidently meant, "This represents my body." Likewise He took one of the Passover cups and passed it around with the explanation, "This is my blood which ratifies the covenant, the blood which is poured out for many for the forgiveness of their sins" (Williams). The covenant was the new covenant (see Jer. 31:31-34); the new covenant would be ratified by blood as the old one had been. The term for covenant does not express an agreement between equal parties but an arrangement sovereignly ordered by God; man may accept or reject it at his peril. "For many" *(on behalf of* or *instead of* many) clearly teaches the substitutionary nature of Christ's death, to the end that sins may be forgiven.

6. *Prophecy of failure and denial* (26:31-35). At the conclusion of the Passover-Lord's Supper, Jesus and the disciples sang a hymn, no doubt a portion of the *Hallel* (Pss. 115-118), and crossed the Kidron Valley to the Mount of Olives. On the way Jesus made a dire prediction of failure on the part of the disciples, especially of Peter's denial. Jesus regarded their forsaking of Him and His demise as a fulfillment of a prophecy recorded in Zechariah 13:7. But He did not leave them hopeless; rather He foretold His resurrection and His meeting with them in Galilee. It is only natural that these Galileans would leave Jerusalem and go back home again after the Crucifixion. Overcome with predictions of Jesus' death and their failure, the disciples disregarded the promise of resurrection and restoration.

Standing strong in his fancied strength, in his self-assurance, Peter declared he would not stumble and fall. Jesus knew better and predicted that before dawn Peter would disown Him three times. But Peter and all the others again made protestations of loyalty.

B. Prelude to the Crucifixion (26:36–27:26)

1. *Agony in the garden* (26:36-46). As Jesus and the disciples went out of Jerusalem to the Mount of Olives, they came to "a place called

Gethsemane," meaning "oil press." This olive grove stood somewhere on the western slope of the Mount of Olives. Because it was a favorite haunt of the apostolic company, Judas knew the place and prepared to come there to seize Jesus (John 18:2). Meanwhile Jesus sought to prepare Himself for the ordeal ahead in an agonizing season of prayer. Entering the garden, He seated eight of the disciples not far from the entrance and took Peter, James, and John deeper into the Garden to "keep watch" with Him, perhaps to provide sympathetic companionship.

Jesus "began to be grieved and distressed." As He was now brought face to face with the horror of bearing the punishment for the sin of the human race, Jesus entered into a whole new emotional state. He shared something of His apprehension with them and sought their support: "My soul is overwhelmed with sorrow to the point of death" (NIV). Then going forward about a stone's throw (Luke 22:41), He prostrated Himself on the ground and "with strong crying and tears" (Heb. 5:7) pled with the Father that if it be His will He would let "this cup pass" from Him. "The most satisfying explanation of the cup refers it to the divine wrath which Christ would incur at the cross as he became man's sin-bearer" (Kent, p. 979).

No human being can ever understand this prayer because we cannot fully comprehend the divine-human nature of Christ. As deity He knew that He must endure the cross and that crucifixion would occur the next day. And as the infinitely Holy One, He knew the horror of bearing sin for the race and the estrangement from the Father. But if He knew the plan of God, how could He pray for salvation to be achieved without His going to the cross? His human nature must have been especially expressing itself here. Immediately He submitted His will to that of the Father (cf. John 5:30; 6:38; Heb. 5:7-8).

Returning to the three, Jesus found them sleeping and said plaintively to self-confident Peter, "So—you had not the strength to finish watching one hour with me?" (Lenski, p. 1039). But His concern was not for Himself even in this trying hour, for He said, "Keep on watching and praying that you may not be tempted." Continue to be alert and to draw upon divine resources lest events surprise you and cause you to yield to temptation. "The spirit," their higher spiritual nature, is willing to express loyalty and service to the Master; but "the flesh," the old nature, is weak and unable to do so.

Three times the Master prayed essentially the same thing, each

time submitting Himself to the will of the Father, and each time finding
the exhausted disciples asleep. The third time He startled them to
alertness: "The time has come" for Him to be betrayed. In fact, "the Son
of man is being betrayed"; the act is in process. "Get up, let us be going,"
not to flee but to meet the betrayer.

2. *Arrest of Jesus* (26:47-56). At that moment Judas came leading a
crowd into the garden. Some had "clubs," temple police; others had
"swords," a band of Roman soldiers (John 18:12); and there were chief
priests and elders (Luke 22:52). Judas had devised a sign that would
identify for the Romans who of those present was Jesus, and he proceeded to identify the Master with the kiss of betrayal. At some point in
the proceedings Jesus asked that His disciples be allowed to go free
(John 18:2-10). All of them did leave (v. 56), but Peter did not go easily.
He meant it when he said he would stay with the Master. Pulling out a
sword, he struck at a slave of the high priest, Malchus by name (John
18:10), and sliced off his ear. Jesus could not tolerate any violence on His
behalf and quickly healed the man completely; the issue never came up
in the subsequent trials. Jesus made it clear that He had at His disposal
the hosts of heaven, but it was not in the plan of God for Him to call on
their defense.

Then Jesus addressed the crowd further, evidently members of the
Sanhedrin or temple police, and protested the manner of His arrest.
They could have taken Him in the temple and need not have seized Him
here like a common robber. But that God's prophetic plan might be
carried out, He voluntarily put Himself in the hands of His captors (John
18:5,8,11), was arrested, and His disciples fled.

3. *Jesus before the Sanhedrin* (26:57-68). After Jesus was bound in
the Garden of Gethsemane, He was led away to Annas, former high
priest, for a preliminary hearing (John 18:12-14,19-24). While that was
going on a hurried call went out to summon the Sanhedrin. When they
had gathered, Jesus was led off to face the reigning high priest,
Caiaphas, son-in-law of Annas, and the Sanhedrin. It is at this point that
Matthew's narrative picks up. Meanwhile Peter also had followed at a
distance and finally had summoned up courage to go to the high priest's
palace, where the meeting of the Sanhedrin was in progress. John had
preceded him there and had gotten inside because he was acquainted
with the high priest. John also was influential in getting Peter admitted
to Caiaphas' palace (John 18:15-18).

Seeking a case against Jesus, the Sanhedrin had brought in "many" witnesses; but their testimony was false and inconsistent and therefore was invalidated (Mark 14:56). Then two witnesses came in to allege that He had claimed He would destroy the temple and in three days build another. This was garbled testimony about a remark Jesus had made three years earlier at the first cleansing of the temple (John 2:19). Such a serious charge normally was a capital offense, but those witnesses failed to provide substantial evidence either.

Finally, in frustration the high priest addressed Jesus Himself, hoping to trap Him with His own statements. First he tried to get Jesus to respond to the witnesses. But Jesus retained a dignified silence. Why should He say anything when the spurious testimony had been self-refuting and nothing further needed to be said? Then the high priest decided to ask Him "under oath" ("adjure"): "Tell us if you are the Christ, the Son of God." Jesus responded in the affirmative but then immediately turned the tables on them. They who were seeking to judge Him would see Him sitting at the right hand of God and coming on the clouds of heaven—sitting as the mighty judge of all peoples.

Then the high priest tore his clothes (certainly not his gorgeous official robes) as a sign of righteous horror and outrage at what he declared to be blasphemy. Possibly this was at least a partially sincere action. After all, anyone who found himself in such abject circumstances without any followers could hardly be the Messiah God had promised His people. Caiaphas put the question of Jesus' guilt to the Sanhedrin and got a unanimous decision of "worthy of death" or deserving to die. Having made their decision, the Sanhedrin engaged in conduct wholly unbecoming to men of their stature. To test Jesus' omniscience and to mock His prophetic office, they blindfolded Him (Luke 22:64) and called on Him to tell who had hit Him. Their violent and despicable conduct may not have discredited Him, but it certainly showed a great deal about their depravity.

4. *Peter's denial* (26:69-75). While the Master was on trial inside Caiaphas' palace, Peter was on trial in the courtyard. The narrative now picks up where it left off in verse 58. As Peter warmed himself in the courtyard, the fire lit up his face enough for him to be recognized. Evidently the portress who had let him in recognized him first: "You also were with Jesus of Galilee" (NIV). "But he denied it," in the language of formal, legal denial used in rabbinical law. Uncomfortable in the light, he moved into the covered archway opening onto the street. Even in the greater darkness he was recognized and again denied knowing Christ

"with an oath," swearing to the truthfulness of his statement. Then about an hour later (Luke 22:59), as Peter tried to lose himself in the crowd in the courtyard, several again accused him of being one of Jesus' followers, "for your accent gives you away" (NIV)—i.e., your Galilean pronunciations.

One of those most vocal on that occasion was a relative of Malchus, servant of the high priest whom Peter had attacked (John 18:26). This time Peter's denial was accompanied by curses, not foul language, but curses to be called down on himself if he were not telling the truth. The NIV gives the true meaning: "Then he began to call down curses on himself and he swore to them, 'I don't know the man!'" Suddenly a rooster crowed and Peter remembered Jesus' prophecy. And apparently at that very moment the Sanhedrin had finished abusing Jesus and were turning Him over to the soldiers in the courtyard. The Lord turned and looked at Peter (Luke 22:61). That look broke him and reduced him to convulsive sobs. Peter fled into the night and dropped completely out of sight until after the Crucifixion.

5. *Second Sanhedrin trial* (27:1-2). To meet the requirement of Jewish law concerning capital crimes, the Sanhedrin held a second session early on Friday morning. Jewish law demanded that in capital cases two trials be held at least a day apart. This meeting sought to ratify the earlier decision and transfer Jesus to Roman authorities with dispatch before a popular rising on His behalf. The Sanhedrin "passed a resolution against Jesus to put him to death" (Lenski, p. 1076). They could do no more because the Romans reserved the right of capital punishment. Having acted against Him, they led Him away to Pilate, the Roman governor who had come from the capital in Caesarea to Jerusalem for the Passover season.

6. *Judas's suicide* (27:3-10). "Then Judas," as he watched the procession form to take Jesus to Pilate and came to realize the consequences of his sin, was filled with remorse and determined to return the blood money to the priests. The thirty pieces of silver became abhorrent to him. The Sanhedrin refused to accept the money and with coldness of heart scorned Judas's confession of having betrayed an innocent man. They tossed off his remorse with the callous, "What is that to us?" They had what they wanted from Judas and were no longer concerned with him or his problems. Totally frustrated, Judas went to the temple and threw the money into the holy place, where only the priests could enter, and went out and hanged himself.

Evidently somewhat later, after the Crucifixion, the priests finally settled their minds enough to dispose of the money. Concluding that it could not be put in the temple treasury, they finally decided to use it to buy "the field of the potter," which subsequently was used as a burial place for "strangers," non-local Jews who died in Jerusalem. The field came to be known as "the field of blood," or "Akeldama" (Acts 1:18-19). Such a burial place must have been Levitically pure ground, and thus it could not have been located in the polluted or morally unclean valley of Hinnom, where tradition now places it. Though the site was well-known in Matthew's day, Roman destruction of Jerusalem in A.D. 70 obliterated many landmarks and its location is now unknown.

Verses 9 and 10 refer to fulfillment of a prophecy in Jeremiah, but the passage actually appears in Zechariah 11:12-13. Resolution of the problem is not easy but may be achieved by viewing Jeremiah as the first book of the Prophets, second part of the Hebrew Bible, as the first section was called the Law and the third part the Psalms. Though Jeremiah was sometimes placed at the head of the Prophets, Isaiah was more commonly placed there. Zechariah was, of course, one of the books in that section. Another attempt at solution sees Matthew as combining Zechariah 11:12-13, Jeremiah 18:2-12, and 19:1-15 and only citing one of the sources. No absolute solution has been found. The prophecy refers to payment of thirty pieces of silver to dispose of Israel's shepherd (which Jesus was) and designates it as a price paid to the potter (for his field).

7. *Jesus before Pilate* (27:11-26). The narrative focuses on Jesus once more as He entered Pilate's judgment hall. Since no charge of blasphemy would impress the Romans, the Sanhedrin changed tactics and presented a list of political charges (Luke 23). The accusation that He claimed to be King of the Jews and was guilty of treason against the Roman government is the only one that got serious attention from Pilate. To the question of whether He was King of the Jews, Jesus answered in the affirmative but then qualified His answer with an explanation of the nature of His kingdom (John 18:34-38). As is also clear from the Gospel of John, the hearing before Pilate was private and ended with the latter's decision that Jesus was innocent of the charges leveled. The Sanhedrin would not stand for acquittal and hurled numerous charges against Jesus when Pilate brought Him back outside to face them. When Jesus remained silent, Pilate was tremendously impressed with His quiet dignity and refused to deal with their false charges.

Among the accusations leveled against Jesus was one of stirring up trouble even in Galilee (Luke 23:5). Grasping at straws in an effort to be rid of this difficult case, Pilate sent Jesus to Herod Antipas, ruler of Galilee, who happened to be in town. After only a brief hearing, Herod returned Jesus to Pilate's jurisdiction and the Roman again found himself in a predicament.

When Pilate was pondering what to do next, a delegation approached him with the request that he honor the custom of releasing a prisoner at Passover time (Mark 15:8). Thinking that if he gave the crowd a choice of the innocent Jesus or a very disreputable prisoner they would choose the former, Pilate presented them the alternative of Jesus or Barabbas. Barabbas was guilty of insurrection—and murder and robbery in the process. Clearly Pilate was trying to put the common people against the Sanhedrin. He understood that the Sanhedrin had launched a vendetta against Jesus because of "envy"; He was too influential with the masses. Evidently at this critical moment Pilate's wife sent an urgent message pleading with him to exonerate Jesus. But while Pilate was absent from his tribunal to receive the message and ponder it briefly, the priests persuaded the crowd to opt for Barabbas; how they did so is not clear. The decision left Pilate stunned and helpless.

Then instead of deciding what to do with Jesus on his own, Pilate in his moment of uncertainty put himself in the hands of the crowd and thus unwittingly in the hands of the Sanhedrin. When Pilate raised the question of what to do with Jesus, presumably the Sanhedrin first, followed by the rest, chanted, "Crucify him" (Mark 15:13). In effect they were saying, "Execute Him." Because the Romans would carry out the execution, which they normally performed by crucifixion, it was natural to urge crucifixion. As the crowd grew more and more ugly, Pilate finally capitulated to them. But he still sought to extricate himself from responsibility for Jesus' death and symbolically washed his hands of guilt in the matter. At that point the people assumed the responsibility and its guilt and in doing so brought upon themselves and their descendants the judgment of God, which often has been evident in the history of Israel. Then Pilate handed Jesus over to be flogged, with the hope that the terrible spectacle would stir sympathy in the crowd and yet save Jesus (John 19:1-5). But his efforts came to naught and the crowd demanded the Crucifixion.

C. The Lord's Death and Burial (27:27-66)

1. *The Crucifixion* (27:27-56). As a prelude to Jesus' crucifixion, the soldiers led Him away into the courtyard of the governor's official residence to make sport of Him there. Since He "claimed" to be a king, He would need a royal robe (a "scarlet cloak," perhaps a cast-off cloak that once had belonged to a Roman soldier), a crown (one of thorns would look ridiculous and could be used to inflict pain), and a scepter. A derisive "Hail, King of the Jews" would do as an imitation imperial salute, and spitting would substitute for the kiss of homage. And they "kept beating Him on His head" with the reed that represented His scepter, to drive the thorns in deeper and inflict pain and to show derision for His royal authority. Finally they took off the mock regalia, put Jesus' own clothes back on Him, and an execution squad of four soldiers led Him out to be crucified (John 19:23).

As the soldiers led Jesus outside the city to the place of crucifixion, His physical strength finally gave out. Since He was no longer able to carry His own cross, they "impressed" a certain "Simon of Cyrene" and forced him to carry it. Simon was a Jew from Cyrene, now a part of Libya, who apparently had moved to Jerusalem and attended a synagogue along with other Jews from Cyrene (Acts 2:10; 6:9).

At length the procession came to a place called "Golgotha," or "place of a skull." The English word "Calvary" comes from the Latin *calvaria*, "a skull." Golgotha seems to have been a slight knoll with a smooth rounded top which resembled a bald head or skull. Evidently it was a well-known place on the north or northwest of the city just outside the city wall. The two suggestions for the location of Golgotha are the Church of the Holy Sepulcher and Gordon's Calvary. Continuing discoveries help to give the former an excellent claim to being the very spot of Golgotha, while the latter, popularized as the site of the Crucifixion late in the nineteenth century, does not have much to support its claim. Perhaps neither is the true place.

Before the act of crucifixion, the soldiers kept offering Jesus wine mixed with myrrh, which had a stupifying effect and which made it easier for the executioners to handle condemned persons. But He repeatedly refused (literal Greek) to drink, wishing to have all His faculties unclouded as He assumed His task of bearing the sin of the whole world. Then they crucified Him; none of the Gospels tell how, but they only specify that both His hands and feet were nailed to the cross (John 20:25; Luke 24:39-40) and not merely tied there. The cross was not raised high above the crowd; His feet would have been only two to three feet above ground.

Commonly a placard ("superscription") was placed above the head of a condemned man and attached to the upright pole of the cross, bearing the name of the criminal and his crime. In this case His name was given as "Jesus of Nazareth" (John 19:19) and His crime as "King of the Jews" (His claim). Pilate refused to say merely that "He claimed to be King of the Jews," even though the chief priests protested the wording (John 19:21-22).

"Then" two robbers were crucified with Jesus, one on either side. Evidently they were guilty of more than thievery because theft was not a capital offense. Likely they were involved in the same conspiracy as Barabbas (Mark 15:7). The clothes of the condemned fell to the soldiers, who parted Jesus' outer cloak into four parts along the seams and cast lots for the inner seamless garment of linen. The reference to fulfillment of the prophecy of Psalm 22:18, appearing in verse 35, does not occur in the best manuscripts and seems to have been introduced from John 19:24, where it is genuine. Then the executioners sat down and guarded the site; in this they were aided by a detachment of soldiers able to handle either those who might seek to free the condemned or to mutilate them.

"Those passing by" could refer to people of the city who were passing by this public execution place. But the nature of their taunts may indicate that they were a little better informed than the mob in general. Reference to destruction of the temple and rebuilding it in three days was a charge leveled earlier by members of the Sanhedrin or their attendants (26:61). "Kept blaspheming" is the literal translation and shows they were not merely defaming a criminal but were actually blaspheming the Son of God.

Verse 39 may not refer to any members of the Sanhedrin, but verse 41 certainly does. The chief priests, scribes, and elders mocking among themselves or addressing the crowd said, "He saved others," at least is alleged to have done so, "himself he cannot save," a fact which cast doubt on all His claims. But in this statement lies the essence of the gospel. If Jesus Christ is to save others from their sins, He cannot save Himself from death; only His substitutionary sacrifice could provide salvation for others. Even if He had come down from the cross, they would not have believed. And when He rose from the dead, they refused to believe it and did all they could to suppress news of the fact.

From the "sixth hour," noon, until the "ninth hour," 3:00 P.M., darkness settled over "all the land," how far beyond the area of Jerusalem is not clear. During all that time a blanket of silence covered Jesus' sufferings. Finally He cried out in Aramaic, "Eli, Eli, lama sabachthani," which is rendered in Greek for Greco-Roman readers: "My God, my God, for what purpose did you forsake me?" (from Ps. 22:1, one of the greatest messianic psalms).

This quote gives a clue as to what was going on during these awful hours of darkness. The Son was being made sin for us (2 Cor. 5:21; Gal. 3:13), and He was suffering the penalty human beings deserved—estrangement from God. As a human being He did not cry "my Father" but "my God." And He did not ask why the penalty or judgment had to fall but rather "what purpose" was served in its coming in this way. Some from the crowd either mistakenly or derisively interpreted "Eli" to be a cry for Elijah.

Apparently at this point Jesus said, "I thirst" (John 19:28), and a soldier dipped a sponge in a jar of wine vinegar and held it on a stick for Jesus to drink. Jesus sucked on the sponge briefly (John 19:30); this time the wine offered was not mixed with a drug. No doubt the wine was from a jar kept for the soldier's own use. Then Jesus cried out in a loud voice, evidently the trumpet cry of John 19:30, "It is finished," and He died.

Matthew next commented on some events and people connected with the death of Jesus. First, the veil or curtain between the holy place and holy of holies in the temple was torn in two from top to bottom, symbolizing the opening of God's presence to believers by the atoning death of Christ (Heb. 6:19-20; 10:19-22). Second, there was earthquake action. Third, many Old Testament saints arose from the dead, symbolizing Christ's victory over death. And after Christ's resurrection they appeared to many in Jerusalem as a witness to His resurrection. What happened to these people subsequently is not stated; perhaps they were translated to heaven.

Fourth, the centurion (commander of a contingent of 100 men) in charge of the Crucifixion concluded on the basis of all he had observed, "Truly this was God's Son" (cf. Mark 15:39). Perhaps he came to full belief in Christ, as tradition says he did. Apparently some of his men were equally affected by what they had seen, but to what degree is not clear. Fifth, Mark commented on some women watching from a distance: Mary of Magdala on the western shore of the Sea of Galilee, Mary the mother of James the less and Joses, and Salome, the wife of Zebedee and mother of James and John. These women "ministered" to Him in Galilee (cf. Luke 8:1-3), no doubt providing sums for the common treasury which Judas had supervised. They became significant witnesses to the death, burial, and resurrection of Jesus.

2. *The burial of Jesus* (27:57-66). "Evening having come," the first evening from mid-afternoon to sunset, Joseph of Arimathea rushed out to get permission to bury Jesus. Jewish custom required burial before sunset, even of criminals. And since this was Friday, the day of "the Preparation" for Sabbath (Mark 15:42), it was necessary to conclude activities earlier than usual. Matthew does not go into detail on how Pilate had to satisfy himself that Jesus was indeed dead and that Nicodemus was involved in the burial activities (cf. Mark 15:42-47; John 19:38-42). Joseph buried Jesus in his own new tomb and closed the entrance with a large stone. Mary Magdalene and Mary the mother of Joses were witnesses of the location of the tomb and were important testimony to the fact that the right tomb was empty on resurrection morning.

Apparently on Sabbath morning the high priests and some Pharisees became concerned about the aftermath of Jesus' death. They remembered that Jesus had talked about rising again in three days; how they knew that we do not know. Though they did not believe Jesus would rise, they wanted to prevent the disciples from taking the body and spreading stories about resurrection. The Pharisees, who believed in resurrection from the dead and taught the people to believe in it, were especially afraid the populace might accept such a report if it were circulated. So they won Pilate's permission to station soldiers at the tomb and make it as secure as they could to prevent any "deception." It is interesting to note that after the death of Jesus His enemies were worried about the idea of His resurrection, but the dejected disciples apparently had forgotten about the promise.

For Further Study

1. What reasons can you discover for Judas's decision to forsake and ultimately to betray Jesus?

2. What details about the Lord's Supper that do not appear in Matthew can you glean from parallel accounts in the Gospels?

3. From a study of all the Gospels try to reconstruct in detail the scene in the Garden of Gethsemane.

4. What sort of person do you think Pilate really was?

Chapter 14

The Triumph of the Messiah
(Matthew 28:1-20)

A. The Resurrection (28:1-10)

Jesus had paid the penalty for sin. There was no longer any reason for Him to remain in the tomb. His resurrection provided the assurance that the penalty had indeed been paid. Moreover, it furnished the basis for our resurrection (1 Cor. 15) and eventuated in the entrance into heaven of our ever-living Intercessor who pleads our case before the Father on the basis of His finished work at Calvary (Heb. 7:25; Rom. 8:31-34).

The Gospel writers did not dwell on the gory details of the Crucifixion or the glorious aspects of the Resurrection in an effort to evoke an emotional response of sympathy or exhilaration. Our faith rests on historical facts, not on emotional experience. We must be careful that emotive responses are based on and flow from a proper and intelligent perception of the facts of Christianity and are not a substitute for such perception.

It is remarkable how the accounts of the Resurrection in the four Gospels substantially agree and yet extensively diverge in details. The differences demonstrate that the Gospels are independent of one another and did not copy from one another as scholars often assert. A combination of all the accounts of the Resurrection reveals the following probable order of appearances of the risen Messiah:

1. To Mary Magdalene (Mark 16:9-11; John 20:11-18)
2. To the women (Matt. 28:8-10)
3. To Peter on resurrection afternoon (Luke 24:34; 1 Cor. 15:5)
4. To the two on the road to Emmaus (Mark 16:12; Luke 24:13-32)

5. To the ten disciples (minus Thomas) on resurrection evening (Luke 24:36-43; John 20:19-25)
6. To the eleven disciples a week later (John 20:26-31; 1 Cor. 15:5)
7. To seven disciples by the Sea of Galilee (John 21:1-23)
8. To about 500 (Matt. 28:16-20; Mark 16:15-18; 1 Cor. 15:6)
9. To James (1 Cor. 15:7)
10. To the group at the Ascension (Mark 16:19-20; Luke 24:44-53; Acts 1:3-12)

"After the Sabbath" (28:1), on Sunday about dawn, a group of women, including Mary Magdalene, Mary the mother of James, Salome, Joanna (Luke 24:10), and others, went to the tomb to anoint Jesus' body (Mark 16:1-2). As they approached, an earthquake occurred and an angel descended and rolled back the great stone from the entrance, not to let Jesus out, but to let witnesses in to verify the Resurrection. Actually the Scripture does not say when Jesus rose from the dead; no doubt it was prior to the visit of the women. Apparently as soon as Mary Magdalene realized that the body of Jesus was gone, and before the announcement of the Resurrection, she ran off to tell Peter and John that His body was missing (John 20:1-2).

The other women reacted more slowly. Evidently somewhat earlier the angel had not only rolled the great circular stone from its groove in front of the tomb entrance but also had tipped it back away from the entrance and had sat on it. The shock of his supernatural brilliance and the earthquake rendered the Roman guard temporarily unconscious.

The angel then apparently went inside the tomb where he joined another angel; so when the women entered they saw two angels (Luke 24:3-4), but only one seems to have been vocal. When the women entered, they did not have to state their mission (Mark 16:5); the supernatural messengers told them why they had come, announced the Resurrection, and invited them to inspect the place where Jesus had lain. No doubt they saw the linen strips in which He had been tightly wrapped (John 20:5-6), which certainly would not have been left behind if His body had been snatched away. Then the angel commanded them to go quickly and tell the disciples to meet Jesus in Galilee as He had previously announced (Matt. 26:32).

The women rushed off obediently. Apparently Mary Magdalene then followed Peter and John to the tomb and was rewarded with the first resurrection appearance (John 20:11-18). Then it seems Jesus appeared to the rest of the women, after they had seen the disciples, received their worship, and gave them the same message that the angels had given them earlier (v. 7; Luke 24:9-11).

B. Report of the Soldiers (28:11-15)

Probably before the women arrived (v. 11), the Roman soldiers regained consciousness and fled to the city. What happened next Matthew especially could be expected to report. Writing for a Jewish audience, he would desire to expose the false report about the Resurrection circulating among the Jews. The soldiers, turned over to the Sanhedrin by Pilate (27:65-66), reported to Jewish rather than Roman authorities.

The Sanhedrin met and voted a handsome bribe to persuade the soldiers to spread a story to the effect that the disciples had stolen Jesus' body while they were sleeping. What an incredible story! How could the soldiers know what happened while they were asleep? And how could the whole contingent be so soundly asleep that the disciples could break the seal and move such a large stone and steal the body without waking them up? And what honorable Roman soldier would have fallen asleep at his post of duty and then publicly incriminated himself for dereliction of duty? Yet the story was spread and some still believe it. As part of the bargain the Sanhedrin committed themselves to satisfy Pilate about their conduct—by whatever means it took.

C. The Great Commission (28:16-20)

Commentators commonly identify the meeting with the disciples described here as identical with the appearance to more than 500 referred to in 1 Corinthians 15:6. By this time Jesus had appeared to the disciples twice already in Jerusalem and did not need to appear to them again, exclusively, in faraway Galilee. But certainly the Eleven were among the 500. This was a significant meeting, announced three times (26:32; 28:7,10). Some of those present still "doubted." Whether doubters were among the Eleven or a larger group cannot be certainly determined.

During this encounter Jesus made an astounding and comprehensive claim: "All authority has been given to Me in heaven and on earth" (NASB)—over all the hosts of heaven and the evil spirit world and all on earth, both friend and foe. That comprehensive authority stands behind the following commission. The literal command is to "disciple all people"—to evangelize them and to enlist them in the great band of

Christ's followers; to baptize them, to administer the rite by which people publicly acknowledge commitment to Christ, and to do so in a distinctively Christian manner (in the name of Father, Son, and Holy Spirit); and to teach them, not only to impart a full knowledge of the truth of God, but to urge an obedience to that truth in daily conduct (to "observe").

Though the task is great, so are the resources: "I am with you always." The infinitely powerful One is present to guard; the infinitely wise One is present to impart wisdom; the infinitely loving One is present to provide every need and dress every wound. "To the end of the age"; the Infinite One can be counted on to make abundant provision until He comes again.

For Further Study

1. In a Bible encyclopedia or Bible dictionary, study the nonbiblical theories of the Resurrection: e.g., swoon theory, vision theory, stolen body theory.

2. Can you suggest any reasons why Jesus should have appeared to Mary Magdalene first after the Resurrection?

3. How do you fit into the Great Commission?

4. We often talk about the importance of the Resurrection for the Christian faith, but what did it mean to Jesus?

Bibliography

Alford, Henry. *The Greek Testament.* Revised by Everett F. Harrison. Chicago: Moody Press, 1958.

Argyle, A. W. *The Gospel According to Matthew.* Cambridge: Cambridge University Press, 1963.

Atkinson, Basil F. C. "The Gospel of Matthew." *The New Bible Commentary.* Rev. ed. Edited by F. Davidson and others. Grand Rapids: Wm. B. Eerdmans Publishing Company, 1954.

Barclay, William. *The Gospel of Matthew.* 2nd ed. Philadelphia: Westminster Press, 1958.

Bruce, Alexander B. *The Synoptic Gospels. The Expositor's Greek Testament.* Reprint ed. Grand Rapids: Wm. B. Eerdmans Publishing Company, n.d.

Carr, A. *The Gospel According to St. Matthew.* Cambridge: Cambridge University Press, 1887.

English, E. Schuyler. *Studies in the Gospel According to Matthew.* New York: Our Hope, 1935.

Erdman, Charles R. *The Gospel of Matthew.* Philadelphia: Westminster Press, 1948.

Gibson, John M. *The Gospel of St. Matthew. The Expositor's Bible.* Reprint ed. Grand Rapids: Wm. B. Eerdmans Publishing Company, 1943.

Harrison, Everett F. *Introduction to the New Testament.* Rev. ed. Grand Rapids: Wm. B. Eerdmans Publishing Company, 1971.

Hiebert, D. Edmond. *An Introduction to the New Testament.* Vol. 1. Chicago: Moody Press, 1975.

Hobbs, Herschel H. *An Exposition of the Gospel of Matthew.* Grand Rapids: Baker Book House, 1965.

Jamieson, Robert; Fausset, Andrew R.; and Brown, David. *A Commentary, Critical, Experimental and Practical on the Old and New Testaments.* Reprint ed. Grand Rapids: Wm. B. Eerdmans Publishing Company, 1945.

Kent, Homer A., Jr. "Matthew." *The Wycliffe Bible Commentary.* Chicago: Moody Press, 1962.

Kuen, Alfred F. *I Will Build My Church.* Chicago: Moody Press, 1971.

Lange, John P. *The Gospel According to Matthew.* Reprint ed. Grand Rapids: Zondervan Publishing House, n.d.

Lenski, R. C. H. *The Interpretation of St. Matthew's Gospel.* Columbus: The Wartburg Press, 1943.

Lloyd-Jones, D. Martyn. *Studies in the Sermon on the Mount.* Grand Rapids: Wm. B. Eerdmans Publishing Company, 1959.

Macaulay, Joseph C. *After This Manner.* Grand Rapids: Wm. B. Eerdmans Publishing Company, 1952.

Robert, A., and Feuillet, A. *Introduction to the New Testament.* New York: Desclee Company, 1965.

Scroggie, W. Graham. *A Guide to the Gospels.* London: Pickering & Inglis, 1948.

Tasker, R. V. G. *The Gospel According to St. Matthew.* Grand Rapids: Wm. B. Eerdmans Publishing Company, 1961

Tenney, Merrill C. *The Genius of the Gospels.* Grand Rapids: Wm. B. Eerdmans Publishing Company, 1951.

Unger, Merrill F. *Unger's Bible Handbook.* Chicago: Moody Press, 1966.

Vincent, Marvin R. *Word Studies in the New Testament.* Vol. 1. Reprint ed. Grand Rapids: Wm. B. Eerdmans Publishing Co., 1946.

Vos, Howard F. *Beginnings in the Life of Christ.* Chicago: Moody Press, 1975.

Walvoord, John F. *Matthew: Thy Kingdom Come.* Chicago: Moody Press, 1974.

Listed below are Bible translations specifically referred to in this study.

Beck, William F. *The New Testament in the Language of Today.* St. Louis: Concordia Publishing House, 1964.

New American Standard Bible. La Habra, Calif.: The Lockman Foundation, 1960. Referred to in this study as NASB.

New International Version, New Testament. New York: New York Bible Society, 1973. Referred to in this study as NIV.

The Holy Bible. The American Standard Version. Camden, N.J.: Thomas Nelson & Sons, 1901. Referred to in this study as ASV.

The Holy Bible. The Authorized or King James Version. Referred to in this study as KJV.

The Holy Bible. The Revised Standard Version. New York: Thomas Nelson & Sons, 1946. Referred to in this study as RSV.

Williams, Charles B. *The New Testament: A Private Translation in the Language of the People.* Chicago: Moody Press, 1949.